The Power of RISKY PLAY in the Early Years

ZOE SILLS & SARAH WATKINS

The Power of RISKY PLAY in the Early Years

Sage

1 Oliver's Yard
55 City Road
London EC1Y 1SP

2455 Teller Road
Thousand Oaks
California 91320

Unit No 323-333, Third Floor, F-Block
International Trade Tower
Nehru Place, New Delhi – 110 019

8 Marina View Suite 43-053
Asia Square Tower 1
Singapore 018960

Editor: Amy Thornton
Senior project editor: Chris Marke
Cover design: Wendy Scott
Typeset by: C&M Digitals (P) Ltd, Chennai, India
Printed and bound by CPI Group (UK) Ltd, Croydon, CR0 4YY

Library of Congress Control Number: 2024951342

British Library Cataloguing in Publication data

A catalogue record for this book is available from the British Library

ISBN 978-1-5296-8582-4
ISBN 978-1-5296-8581-7 (pbk)

For all of you who recognise how remarkable children are and how important play is.

Sarah

For the wonderful members of my 'tribe' – the outdoor learning community friends who have supported me on this journey and beyond. For my husband – my roots and my rock, always believing in me. For our daughter, whose existence led me to find a new path and dare to dream of new adventures.

Zoe

Contents

Acknowledgements

Thank you to every practitioner who collaborated with me on the case studies for the book. Your expertise is truly appreciated.

Sarah

Thank you to everyone I spoke to, from the wonderful world of Early Years and outdoor learning and play professionals to parents and friends who have engaged with me in conversations, sharing some of your stories and wisdom for this book.

Zoe

About the authors

Zoe Sills is a Forest School leader who delivers training and outdoor learning opportunities as Jackdaw Forest School, as well as working for Play Scotland as an Outdoor Play and Learning (OPAL) mentor. She is also the Play Director for the Scottish Outdoor Learning Association. Previously, Zoe has been a pastoral leader, secondary and middle school teacher and manager of Early Years settings.

Sarah Watkins is a Forest School leader who runs an outdoor learning company called Dandy Lions. Sarah was previously Head of School and is now an Associate Lecturer at the University of Worcester, in the Education department.

About this book

The research shows that children need to run, climb, dig, swing, roll, and push the boundaries. Picking up this book shows your commitment to enabling children to play in the way they need to. In the following chapters you'll find useful advice about what constitutes risk in play, why it is beneficial, how to support it, how to risk assess it, and how to support staff to support children on their journey.

We'd like to leave the final word in this section to Ingrid Wilkinson, mother of Billy Bolt, winner of world championships in one of the most dangerous sports in the world. Enduro riders must travel at high speeds over difficult terrain in remote areas, often in challenging weather conditions.

"As parent to a four-time world champion who is living his dream, I dread to think what his life might have become if he had been raised by adults who were risk averse. I applied one key element to Billy's life and that was trust.

Billy wasn't born with resilience, endurance, strength and the ability to ride a bike, he developed these skills over time. His father and I trusted his ability to risk assess a situation and we gave Billy permission to act on this. If I had stepped in daily and said 'Stop! Don't! Be careful!' I would have been destroying his capacity to work it out for himself. It is the adults who must change, not the child.

Billy was often classed as the wild child, reckless and crazy. He was fearless and driven, but not destructive. What I knew deep inside was that every close encounter he had increased his ability to focus, respond in the moment, concentrate, manage the risk at a deeper level. He developed a relationship with nature, he learned what the environment would enable him to do and what was impossible. His relationship with himself and the world around him developed, his ability to conquer situations grew and his thirst for even more risk increased.

My belief as a parent is to help each of my children develop the skills and capacity to achieve their hopes and dreams, to encourage them to fly as high as they possibly can. At times it makes me nervous. My natural instinct is to step in, stop and protect each one, but by doing this I would be denying them the autonomy of being themselves and reaching their full potential. My job is not to protect, it's to support each one to develop skills for life. A child cannot buy independence – it is developed over time by the situations they encounter.

Mistakes are essential and part of life because they are learning experiences from which we grow. Resilience, competence, confidence, self-regulation, a zest for life, we can help our child develop these skills or we can over protect and allow our own fear and anxiety to limit their capacity for growth."

Part 1

Exploring risky play

In this section, we dig down into risky play, starting with the controversial opinion that we don't like the term 'risky play'! If you work in Early Years, and particularly if you manage staff, it's important to understand what this term means in all its complexity. In this first section, we discuss the context of risk in play, presenting the views of prominent theorists and exploring barriers that can prevent children taking ownership of their own play.

1

What is 'risky play'?

All play can be risky for some children on some level at some time in some circumstances, so really risky play is just play.

Newstead, 2016

This chapter

- The working definitions of risk and of risk in play we will be using through this book
- The value of risk in play
- The 16 play types (as categorised by Bob Hughes, 2006)

What's in a name?

This book is titled to make it clear what we are talking about and therefore easy for you to find. However, we need to start with a confession: we *hate* the phrase 'risky play'! Stay with us and learn why, as well as what we *love* about all things 'play', and why an element of risk in play is so important for development.

The word 'risk' automatically conjures up negative associations. Definitions of risk include words such as 'unsafe', 'risk', 'hazardous', 'dangerous', 'possibility', 'injury' and 'uncertainty'. If we were to list some words used by adults supporting children's play who may not be fully on board with risk being part of play (and remembering that we are talking primarily about children aged from birth to six here), what might that list look like? Here are some words from adults' responses to children's play: 'careful', 'slowly', 'hold', 'high', 'don't', 'make sure', 'gently', 'look', 'carefully', 'wait', 'slow', 'jump', 'fall'.

Reflective questions 1.1

Consider these words.

Do any of the words you see surprise you?

Have you heard or possibly even used them at some point?

Are there words here you would exclude?

Are there words here you would add?

The value of risk

All our most basic human instincts compel us to both avoid danger, and therefore risk, and to protect children from harm. So why then is this book *encouraging* risk for our most precious loved ones? Not only that, but in the case of Early Years practitioners and teachers, the most precious loved ones of others? If this is the point where you are nodding along, perhaps engaging in a little eye-rolling, muttering under your breath something about irresponsible writing, etc. – keep reading! This is where we start to make it make sense!

While our adult human instinct to protect our youngest loved ones from harm takes over, we are forgetting – because we were not necessarily aware of it in ourselves – that a child is hardwired for risk. Why? Because everything is a risk when it is new, uncharted territory. New words, new foods, new friends, new school, new playground, new experiences – travelling on things with wheels that we are allowed to propel ourselves, that we have control over; being tall enough to access the climbing wall, tall enough to ride the bigger fairground rides; being strong enough to climb the tree, able to swing ourselves, hang upside down, roll down the hill; having endless energy …

Reflective questions 1.2

What's the last risky thing you did?

It may be easier to think of it in these terms: when did you last feel scared, or even a bit nervous?

Figure 1.1 A child playing on a tree swing

Chances are that the first examples that came to mind are physical situations, but it could be a social or work situation. Perhaps a difficult conversation? Learning a new language? Meeting new people? Meeting the prospective in-laws? Balancing three boxes of eggs on one arm because you couldn't face a second trip to the car to unload the shopping? A new haircut or clothing style? Joining a gym? Joining a choir? A job interview?

We all take risks, all the time. One thing is true, whether the risk-taker is under the age of five or significantly over – what constitutes a risk is different for different people. It is very much an individual measure. There is no *more* or *less*, no *better* or *worse* when it comes to risk. There is only *different*. It is not something that is age and stage related, rather it is entirely personality-linked. In children, it may be that one three-year-old is taking a risk by just sitting on the swing. For another, they love to swing as high as possible, shrieking with glee and shouting 'higher!' every time. Another truth about risk is that our perception of it changes as we get older. And this element *is* age and stage related. The wider our field of experiences, the more we understand about cause-and-effect relationships. The more we understand about what *could* happen, the more we might be inclined to adapt our approach. It is important to remember, however, that the first truth still stands – our personality will ultimately dictate how much of a risk-taker we become.

So, back to this phrase 'risky play' then. Given everything that has been said above, could it in fact be said that what we are talking about is just simply *play*?

Types of play

It can be useful when observing play to be able to identify different behaviours and to recognise what children are learning as they explore different ways of playing. There are many different types of play and there have been numerous attempts to categorise them. For the purposes of this book, we will be referring to the play types categorised by Bob Hughes (2006):

- *creative play*: making, printing, manipulating materials, loose parts;
- *exploratory play*: physically exploring an environment – height, distance, jumping, climbing, swinging; exploring elements; 'what if?';
- *mastery play*: relationship with physical properties – growing, digging, building and destroying/knocking down; controlling elements – fire and water;
- *object play*: playing with any object in different ways; schema;
- *communication play*: singing, rhyming, imitation, slang; non-verbal communication – face and hand gestures, body language;
- *dramatic play*: song and dance, mime, making plays, acting out scenarios – real and imagined;
- *socio-dramatic play*: dramatisation of everyday events or scenarios, often includes reimagining adults' conversations, roles, jobs;
- *role-play*: enacting adult behaviours, imitating mannerisms, voices or dress; play-acting job roles;
- *social play*: interactive play with others, e.g. conversations, negotiations, discussing plan or rules, playing boardgames;
- *rough-and-tumble play*: play fighting, wrestling, jostling, playful pushing and shoving, rolling together; often includes lots of laughter;
- *locomotor play*: movements – chase, tag, hide and seek, climbing, jumping, swinging, racing, ball games;
- *deep play*: focus and engagement in activities with risks or potential danger, taking known risks;
- *fantasy play*: 'being' another person, character or thing;
- *imaginative play*: imaginary food, people or objects which form key parts of play; objects presented as other items;

- *recapitulative play*: play set in past times or taking on historical roles/stories; rituals; war or weapon play; often involves costume and props;
- *symbolic play*: items represent specific places or messages.

A useful resource summarising the play types is the poster in Figure 1.2, produced by Play Scotland.

Figure 1.2 A Playworker's Taxonomy of Play Types *by Bob Hughes, reproduced by kind permission of Play Scotland*

Children don't name their types of play, of course; they are just playing. If asked what they were playing they might tell us a story about it, or just state very factually what is happening. However, if we consider each type of play as adults, we can see that almost every type of play has a risky element. I will at this point highlight my personal issue with the image used for rough-and-tumble play – even as a staunch advocate of play with risk, I draw a line at the idea of a child landing on their head on a trampoline. I will go so far as to say trampolines give me the risky collywobbles … but that's a discussion for later.

Hopefully, what you see highlighted here, is that children should experience each of these play types. It should also be evident that most of these play experiences come with an element of risk, to a greater or lesser extent. As educators of children (and that includes parents, who are a child's first teacher), we have a responsibility to facilitate these opportunities for children. We should be providing experiences for children that meet their developmental needs and the opportunity to choose those they feel comfortable with exploring – children should not be forced to play in a risky way, but will find their own level of challenge.

In section 3.1 of Education Scotland's *Realising the Ambition, Being Me* (2020), the importance of physical development is clearly stated:

> We all have a sensory system called the vestibular system which gives us our sense of balance and spatial awareness. It helps us coordinate our large and fine motor movements and maintain our posture. The development of movement and coordination for a child is linked to communication and cognitive development. For instance, a young child with a developing vestibular system will find it almost impossible to sit still for any length of time or possess the fine motor skills and coordination required for writing before they are ready. This is why observations of a children's actions are crucial to inform our practice and ensure it is developmentally appropriate. The best way to help babies and young children develop this system is through providing daily opportunities for physical play, especially outdoors.

Here we begin to tread on the toes of the benefits (of what we are *not* calling 'risky play'), and that is a whole other chapter. But you see the connection? Play *must*, in order to deliver on the developmental aspect, include an element of risk.

Learning and play

Children learn through play. Depending on your wider reading, play and learning can be seen as being one and the same entity or, alternately, be viewed as different entities. Whatever your preferred definition, they are undoubtedly intrinsically linked. Children also play and learn through exploring. They explore their environment, wherever that may be. Niki Buchan (2018) brings the themes of play and learning together rather beautifully when she writes: 'Play is the natural way a child responds to their environment. They will attempt to play in even the most structured places not designed for play such as escalators, classrooms, shopping malls and airports – often much to the frustration of the adult' (p. 1). News reports of refugees talk of children finding ways to play on beaches, ferries and in tented refugee camps, and Ukrainian children playing in bunkers underground. The need is innate and inescapable.

Figure 1.3 Refugee children playing

Children are not consciously playing in order to learn (although it is true that through play children learn about the world). Rather the learning is a bonus outcome of the process of play. We know that play is voluntary, intrinsically motivated and 'apparently purposeless', or done entirely for its own sake. It is where we explore what we are capable of and what the limits of ourselves and our environment might be. Capability and limits. Risk.

If the opposite of risk – that soft, comfortable, fluffy place that means you don't have to think about all those negative words associated with risk from the list at the start of this chapter – is safe, and safe is, by definition, the absence of harm, then anyone who has raised and/or worked with under sixes has already failed. How many bumps, bruises or worse have the children in your care experienced? Play Wales have produced a fabulous film, *This is Why Play is So Important* (Playful Childhoods, 2023), where a vast cross section of people, from very young children to adults of every age talk about the importance of play to them. The overriding theme throughout the film is play with risk. Risk features in all the footage, and the vast majority of the memories. Adults speak fondly of how they broke their wrists (both of them) jumping from a slide, the feeling of flying through the air when jumping from a swing, the failure to clear the gap between the roofs of two buildings, clearly overridden by the exhilaration of the game (and the indelible memory of their friends laughing at their expense).

Reflective question 1.3

Cast your mind back to your own childhood for a moment – what are your overriding memories of play?

For the vast majority of us, at least some of the more stand-out memories will be outside, most likely away from adults and likely involving an element of risk. For me and my best friend it would be roller-skating. We lived on a hill, that was also a no-through-road, so we had the luxury of being able to play out on the road a lot. We are pretty much polar opposites in character – me the adventurous one, her the home bird – but, at this stage in our lives, we were well matched in our adventures through play and in our abilities on a pair of roller skates. The top was steep, then it levelled out in the middle, with a decent space to slow down, before then continuing on another steep, down-hill section near the bottom. Further up the hill we started, and further down the hill we stopped – I'm pretty sure with the help of the lampposts, or the garden walls of understanding neighbours. However, once we'd cracked hurtling at break-neck speed all the way from the top, stopping in the middle seemed like a waste of energy and opportunity, so we took the natural next step and just kept going. Though not a main road, the road that passed the bottom of ours was a through road, with no possible way for us to see or be seen as we careered down. If we took to the pavement we risked mowing down an unsuspecting pedestrian. Given that there were a relatively high proportion of more elderly (they were probably in their 40s+, but that was positively ancient to us) people in our locale and we were responsible youngsters who always considered others as per our Brownie Promise, we kept to the road. Neither of us is sure to this day how one of us didn't end up under a car, or worse (as the Biffa lorry was a regular visitor to the farm at the top of our road), but we did survive.

My worst injuries were sustained falling off a bike as a child when I took a curb at too close an angle, and later breaking my wrist on a trampoline (see – I hate trampolines). I remember being proud of my scabs and who had the biggest, we wore them like badges of honour. I see my daughter and her friends do the same in the playground now. I have not kept my daughter 'safe' in that respect. The weekly (and the rest) head-bump letters I receive home attest that neither has her school. And I am so happy to know that my internal knot of fear when I see her flying through the air attempting round-offs and free cartwheels, climbing to the top of the highest climbing frame we can find (Mum! Can we stop here? That park had a *huge* climbing frame, I have to try it!) and freewheeling on her bike or skateboard has *not* been picked up on by her, and that I haven't inhibited her sense of adventure, her need to explore, to test her limits and find out what she is capable of. I am not immune to the fear and to the 'what if ...?' possibilities of risk. I have had to learn, as I have learned about the importance of risk for myself, how to prioritise the benefits and the positive opportunities. As Ian Stewart, father of Edinburgh stunt cyclist Danny Stewart says, 'You cannot eliminate risk, so you have got to teach kids how to manage it' (2017).

Figure 1.4 First skateboarding attempt

What is risk?

So now we need to get to the meat of it – what actually is a risk? And, the thing is, a risk is not actually a *thing* at all. A risk is a judgement. It is entirely subjective. That is to say, it is based entirely on the personal feelings/influences of the person looking at it. The thing they are looking at is a hazard – that is the thing that could potentially cause harm. So, whether play can be considered risky depends, firstly, on what hazards exist in that particular type of play and, secondly, on what observing adults deem the worst that could happen. If we agree, from earlier paragraphs, that we cannot prevent every bump or bruise, how do we make this judgement? Do we agree that a little bleeding is OK (think scab competitions – who are we to deprive children of the right to that playground badge of honour?), but broken bones are a no? If that were the agreed benchmark, then nobody would be able to jump from a height of more than about 10cm, as that was how high the step was that my friend at university jumped down and broke both bones in her lower leg in week one. If the judgement was mine there would be no trampolines, except under very strict controls. No, I will never get over it. And actually, that's OK. As play facilitators it is not only OK, but also vital that we are honest about the things that make us uncomfortable.

Ellen Beate Sandseter is the undisputed queen of using the term 'risky play'. There is absolutely a place for the term when you simply want everyone to get what you mean, no faffing around with definitions. Her 2007 study 'Categorising risky play' established six categories:

1. play with great heights;
2. play with high speed;
3. play with harmful tools;
4. play near dangerous elements;
5. rough-and-tumble play; and
6. play where the children can 'disappear'/get lost.

Two further categories were later added by Rasmus Kleppe et al. (2017):

7. play with *impact*;
8. *vicarious* play.

> A small-scale observational study with children from five childcare settings with differing characteristics was undertaken to explore the occurrence and characteristics of risky play for children under four years of age, in relation to the current understanding of risky play. The study found similarities across the different contexts, which seemed to reflect the characteristics of risky play for children aged one to three years. The findings suggest that the existing definition and characteristics of risky play are appropriate for two- and three-year-old children, but for one-year-olds, the study found discrepancies indicating deviations from existing definitions.
>
> Kleppe et al., 2017

Sandseter is a leading expert and recognised worldwide for her research and promotion of the value of risk in playgrounds and play experiences for children. We would argue, very respectfully, that the words 'harmful' [tools] and 'dangerous' [elements] should be removed from that list of categories. Tools are only harmful if used incorrectly or will only cause as much injury as an equally sharp stick, fence or other potential hazard. Elements – fire, water, wind – are as equal in wonder as they are in danger. Like tools, they are to be respected for their power and potential and managed well. Coming from a Forest School background though, where risk is one of the principles and tools and fire are key learning experiences, that is where my judgement might be different from another. Most children are taught to swim in order to make their experiences with water less risky – so it should be for all the elements in nature.

So risky play is not only 'just' play. We assert that risk in play is critical to every child, both in terms of their natural exploration of who they are and the world around them, and as a vehicle to learn their capabilities. If all that our children learn about risk is the theory of what *might* happen, then how will they learn enough to truly protect themselves from harm? How will they learn to manage the risks that life presents them with, if we don't give them the tools to recognise risk and assess their own abilities to manage that? How will they learn to trust in their own abilities if we don't trust them to do so?

Case study: what is risk?

Matt Harder is Deputy Chair of the Forest School Association. He is a primary teacher, bushcraft instructor and Forest School trainer and leader with 15 years' experience of facilitating outdoor learning with children from two to 18 years old.

The way I see it, Risk, with a capital R, falls into three main categories. These are ones I see on a regular basis within our Forest School and outdoor learning sessions.

There's the typical 'risk-assessment-based risk', which is usually constrained to risks involving physical damage, falling from trees, tool use, accidental (or not) ingestion of 'magic potions' which contain copious amounts of pond water and mud.

These risks often have visible (and sometimes scatological) effects.

The other two types of risk are not always easily apparent:

- risk of failure;
- risk of rejection.

Within my sessions, whether Forest School, Outdoor Learning or Learning Outside the Classroom (LOtC), we encourage opportunities for all three risk types, through the medium of play.

Risky play, to my mind, is the most important element of our sessions because it allows for learners to test boundaries of risk creatively, with collaboration and often without the peskiness of interfering adults. Well-informed adult co-players pose a less significant interference and may actually encourage the development of risky play.

(Continued)

It's important to highlight that 'play' is quite a broad term, spanning role-play to experimentation. Often, we see the role-play and imaginative play shift to the more social, creative and experimental play types as children progress through the year groups. Whichever play type though, there are opportunities to encourage risk.

As an example ...

On a muddy autumn morning, I had a group of ten-year-olds; together we set up a tightrope using ratchet straps. This tightrope started at knee height and gradually increased so that the 'finish line' was at 2 metres high.

Despite having handholds, this was a considerably challenging activity, and one particular girl made it almost all the way to the top. There, she froze, her legs shaking and on the verge of a panic attack. Her friends stood below and coached her, encouraging and praising her bravery. She managed to touch the tree at the finish line and came down, beaming. She came to me and said, 'That was the scariest thing I've ever done, but if I can do that, I can do anything.'

Physically risky, but highly rewarding on completion.

I also had a session where a group of seven-year-olds were trying to cook some pancakes. They had a really difficult time beating the flour and milk together, which led to mouthfuls of raw and unmixed flour in the semi-cooked pancakes. However, through these failures, the children independently decided to improve and vary the recipes and, after many mistakes, the same group successfully made delicious apple doughnuts. Here, failures were integral to the learning process. Success at the first instance may have meant no desire to experiment further.

In a group of five-year-olds, there was an established game of 'ice cream parlour' at the mud kitchen. This involved children making mud ice creams for anyone and everyone in the group, including adults. One week, there was a new child who hadn't been to Forest School before. They hung back and watched from a distance for a considerable time; as I watched, they timidly stepped forward and asked for a chocolate ice cream. Immediately, they were absorbed into the group and became a server, asking people for their orders. Overcoming a risk of rejection solidified social skills and friendships were strengthened by this.

These are just three of numerous examples I've seen where opportunities for risk enabled high rewards, boosting self-esteem and developing learning in Forest School sessions. These three types of risk, applicable to all ages and undeniably part of everyday life, need to be encouraged, so our children are able to face these risks and overcome them.

Key takeaways

- The language we use in relation to risk in play is important
- Risk is present throughout life
- Remember the 16 types of play as categorised by Bob Hughes
- Risk enables learning and development
- Childhood memories frequently involve play with an element of risk
- Hazards cause harm; risk is the potential for the harm to be significant (or not) and is subjective
- Sandseter initially established six categories of risky play
- Children need to experience and recognise different types and levels of risk in order to assess and manage their response

2

The history of risk in play

Play is training for the unexpected.

Dr Marc Bekoff, in Spinka et al., 2001

This chapter

- Risk in play as part of childhood development
- How play has evolved over the years
- The categories of risky play
- Viewpoints of historical and contemporary early childhood theorists
- The evolutionary role of risky play
- The view of the Health and Safety Executive on risky play

The evolution of play

Along with other human behaviours, play has evolved and changed through the centuries. For example, we know that in early human societies children developed motor skills, strength and agility through activities like running, climbing and throwing. In many early societies, children learned practical skills through play, such as making tools – play was a crucial part of survival. They explored their natural surroundings through play, learning about the environment, plants, animals and natural resources.

Sometimes, play had a role in initiation rites, some of which were highly risky. For children, these ceremonies enabled them to transition into adulthood or a new social group.

For example, the Ephebeia was an initiation ceremony for young boys living in ancient Greece where they learned the skills needed to defend their city state. The boys would role-play cultural rituals, dressed in ceremonial attire, acting out different scenarios that helped them understand their new responsibilities (Henderson, 2020).

In the US, the Kachina ceremonies are longstanding ceremonial initiation rites which still take place today, and role-play is a crucial part. During the ceremonies, male children from the Hopi tribes encounter older members of the community who are dressed as Kachina spirits. The children role-play interacting with the Kachina impersonators, learning about cultural values and beliefs, and building a sense of belonging to that community (Wright et al., 2014).

In the UK, the context of play changed at the end of the 19th century when child mortality rates fell dramatically. Earlier in the Victorian period, two-thirds of children died before they reached the age of five, and childhood was seen as a highly dangerous period to be hurried through. Suddenly though, childhood became associated with freedom, creativity, emotion and malleability and people began to think differently about play and children's capacities (Reynolds, 2014).

In the 1980s, Dr David Elkind expressed his concern that children were once again being 'hurried through' childhood, this time by busy, stressed adults who were pushing children to grow up too fast, missing out on vital, active, exploratory play (Elkind, 1981). It seemed to many that children's play was being limited, both in terms of time and what children were permitted to do. Opportunities for risk in play were being curtailed.

Reflective questions 2.1

Can you think of any types of outdoor play that link to survival needs?

Have you observed any yourself?

Dr Ellen Sandseter's categories

As part of the concern that children's unstructured play was being unnecessarily limited, the term 'risky play' started to be used in educational circles. The phrase gained popularity in the early to mid-2010s when Dr Ellen Beate Hansen Sandseter, as mentioned previously, set out her six categories of risky play (see Chapter 1, page 12). The categories were developed through Sandseter's research and her observations of children playing in different ways, which led to her identifying common themes and patterns (2010). Her work became highly influential in highlighting the importance of enabling children to engage in activities that may involve risk for their overall development and well-being.

The views of early childhood theorists on risky play

Risky play is not a new concept. Here we explore the views of early theorists whose work still has resonance today.

Friedrich Froebel

> *To learn a thing in life and through doing is much more developing, cultivating and strengthening than to learn it merely through the verbal communication of ideas.*
>
> Froebel, 1887

Friedrich Froebel, who opened the first kindergarten or 'garden of children' in 1826, recognised that children's brains develop significantly during the first three years of life. He believed that learning was driven by play. Froebel's kindergartens included gardening spaces, animals to care for, nature walk routes and loose natural play materials for exploration. He introduced the concept of *freedom in play* and emphasised the importance of self-directed, exploratory play. Froebel's educational philosophy included the idea that children learn best through direct experience and hands-on activities. He encouraged the use of play materials called *gifts* and *occupations* that supported children to engage in creative and imaginative play. These activities often involved elements of risk – for example, fragile building structures or experimenting with materials that might have unpredictable outcomes. Froebel believed that, by engaging in play with an element of risk, children would develop important skills such as problem-solving, critical thinking and coping skills. He saw play as a means for children to understand the world around them, learn from their experiences and develop a sense of agency and confidence. Froebel's view on risk in play was positive: he saw it as a crucial component of a child's development and a way for them to learn and grow (Froebel, 1887; Ulich et al., 1968).

Dr Maria Montessori

> *The strength of even the smallest children is more than we imagine, but it must have a free play in order to reveal itself.*
>
> Dr Maria Montessori, 1986

In the early 20th century, Dr Maria Montessori developed her method of education, with a strong focus on supporting children to explore and engage with their environment in a hands-on and experiential way. Montessori believed in environments that encourage children to learn through their own exploration and experiences, drawing on their natural curiosity

Figure 2.1 Children make sense of the world by taking risks in play

and independence. She felt that children have a natural desire to take risks, to challenge themselves and to weigh the risk against the benefit. Without opportunities to take risks, according to Montessori, children cannot reach their full potential or even have fulfilling lives.

The emphasis is on creating an environment that enables children to challenge themselves in individual ways rather than intentionally introducing unnecessary risks. Core to the Montessori approach is the belief that children benefit from engaging in activities that challenge them physically, intellectually and emotionally.

Rachel and Margaret McMillan

> *We must open our doors to the toddlers. We must plan the right kind of environment for them and give them sunshine, fresh air and good food.*
>
> Rachel McMillan, in Jarvis and Liebovich, 2015

The McMillan sisters, Rachel and Margaret, also strongly believed that children should have a high level of independence and responsibility as well as opportunities for active, hands-on learning experiences. The McMillan Open Air Nursery School, thought to be the first of its kind in England, opened in 1914; children were encouraged to look after plants and animals. They were supported to learn about the importance of caring for themselves, animals and their peers. The McMillans believed strongly that children learn through child-led exploration, which included play involving risk (Stevinson, 1954).

Reflective question 2.2

These theorists all believe that prolonged time outdoors is crucial.

How can outdoor play support problem-solving and resilience?

Contemporary theories

In more recent times, theorists have continued to discuss risk in play. Here are some prominent views.

Stuart Brown

Psychiatrist and play researcher, Stuart Brown, has written extensively on the importance of play in human development. He stresses the crucial role of play, including risky play, in developing children's creativity, resilience and social skills. In his TED talk, he states that rough-and-tumble play is essential for development:

> Preschool kids, for example, should be allowed to dive, hit, whistle, scream, be chaotic and develop through that a lot of emotional regulation and a lot of the other social byproducts – cognitive, emotional and physical – that come as a part of rough-and-tumble play.
>
> Brown, 2009

Brown believes that self-directed play helps with building cognitive skills, social development and coping with stress. According to Brown, humans are designed to play throughout their whole lifetime, and rough-and-tumble play at an early age can prevent violent behaviour in later life.

Peter Gray

Developmental psychologist Peter Gray proposes that play is self-chosen, self-directed and intrinsically motivated (Gray, 2013). To Gray, play and risk underpin the development of essential life skills:

> 'Play is, among other things, the way that young mammals learn to control their fear and anger so they can encounter real-life dangers, and interact in close quarters with others, without succumbing to negative emotions'.
>
> (Gray, 214)

Studying hunter gatherer tribes, Gray found that risk in play often provided the skills needed in adulthood. He believes there has been a continuous erosion in children's freedom and opportunity to play, partly caused by the spread of irrational fears and a 'schoolish' view of child development (the view that children best learn everything from adults).

Dr Joe Frost

> *Reasonable risks are essential for children's healthy development.*
>
> Dr Joe Frost, 2010

Dr Joe Frost dedicated more than 50 years to researching child development and play and has been called the 'contemporary father of play advocacy'. He continually called for the need for balanced risk in play environments. Frost wrote comprehensively about the connection between poor well-being and the decline in play and believed that the shift to indoor electronic play, the decline of break times, the threats of lawsuits, parental fear of child injury and excessive regulations and testing were to blame. In his later years, Frost emphasised the need for challenging outdoor play environments, and suggested that depriving children of creative, spontaneous play and time in nature verged on abuse. He felt that many play environments don't allow children to play in the way they need to and that adult-designed play spaces rarely match the depth of creativity of children. Frost acknowledged that there is no quick fix and called for multiple, coordinated and preventative approaches. One possible solution, he felt, was to look at adventure playgrounds, where trained playworkers provide an enabling environment where all individual children can play, learn and develop.

Dr Mariana Brussoni

Children need risk, fear and excitement in play.

Dr Mariana Brussoni, in Brussoni et al., 2015

Dr Mariana Brussoni, a Canadian researcher in the field of paediatric injury prevention, highlights the importance of children engaging in risky play and learning to assess risk in play. She believes that outdoor play can help children build important life skills as well as contributing to physical, cognitive and emotional development. She suggests that allowing children to engage in activities that involve some level of risk, such as climbing or exploring, can develop resilience, problem-solving skills and self-confidence. Advocating for a balanced approach to risk in children's play, she encourages parents to be more open to allowing their children to engage in activities that might initially seem risky, but are developmentally beneficial. Brussoni argues that being overly cautious and restricting all forms of risk can hinder children's development. She feels that those designing community spaces need to prioritise environments that are conducive to child-led outdoor play with an element of risk.

Tim Gill

Childhood is becoming undermined by risk aversion.

Tim Gill, 2007

Writer Tim Gill advocates for urban planning and community design that facilitates active, adventurous play. Gill is a prominent advocate for the importance of risk in play for healthy development and calls for a more permissive and supportive attitude towards children engaging in challenging activities. Gill argues that risk is an integral part of play and that children inherently seek out and enjoy activities that involve an element of danger. According to Gill, there are many benefits associated with risk in play, including enhanced physical and emotional development, improved problem-solving skills and increased resilience. He suggests that by facing and overcoming challenges, children develop a sense of mastery and self-confidence, as well as developing a better understanding of their capabilities and limitations. Restricting these activities can hinder their natural development. While Gill advocates for allowing children more freedom in play, he also emphasises the need for a thoughtful approach that recognises and mitigates unnecessary risks without eliminating all challenge. Gill criticises the trend for overprotective parenting and a risk-averse culture and argues that shielding children from all potential risks can deprive them of valuable learning experiences and hinder their ability to assess and manage risks on their own.

Ellen Sandseter and Leif Kennair

> *Children who aren't allowed to take risks are more prone to anxiety conditions later in life. No risk = fear, insecurity, anxiety, lack of self-esteem.*
>
> Ellen Sandseter and Leif Kennair, 2011

Figure 2.2 Children need to learn to assess and manage risks

Dr Ellen Sandseter, who has contributed so much to our understanding of risk in play, collaborated with Leif Kennair on research exploring the evolutionary perspective on children's risky play behaviours. Sandseter and Kennair suggest that risky play evolved to help children tackle normal phobias. It can have a positive impact on children's fear responses, as well as providing children with exhilarating positive emotions. For example, play with great heights can reduce a fear of heights later in life. Play where children can 'disappear' or get lost, such as exploring unknown areas alone, may reduce fear of separation. Through play with risk, children are excited and engaged while learning to master age-appropriate challenges.

Sanseter and Kennair state that if children don't have opportunities for play with risk, the fear responses may persist even when no longer relevant, potentially leading to anxiety disorders. They argue against an exaggerated focus on safety in children's play, emphasising the importance of challenging and adventurous outdoor physical activities where children push their limits and overcome fears. Advocating for a balanced approach, Sandseter and Kennair stress the need to avoid overprotection and, instead, to differentiate between risks and hazards, enabling children to encounter challenges and make choices.

Reflective question 2.3

Can you think of any specific adventurous play activities that might support children in dealing with common childhood fears?

Legislation and safety standards

During my lifetime, there have been significant changes in legislation and safety standards around children's play, informed by research and changing attitudes. We're all familiar with the images of playground equipment from the 1970s that are regularly shared on social media, including high metal slides and hard surfacing. I clearly remember the heat of these slides in the summer, and my sister had to be treated in hospital for concussion after a fall from the top of one. However, I also remember the thrill of finally conquering some of these playground challenges!

In the 1980s and 1990s, the British and European Standards (BS EN) for playground equipment were introduced (BSI Group, 1986), providing guidelines to be followed by playground designers. One significant change was the introduction of safety surfacing to reduce serious injuries from falls. Impact-absorbing surfaces, such as rubber mulch or synthetic turf, underneath play equipment were recommended.

Although we still have a long way to go, there has also been an increased focus on designing playgrounds that are inclusive and accessible to children of all abilities. Guidelines are in place now to ensure that playgrounds accommodate the needs of all children, but there does need to be more consultation of children who have difficulty accessing standard play equipment.

In the late 20th century, particularly in the 1980s and 1990s, there was a shift towards adopting a risk–benefit assessment approach in evaluating playground safety, acknowledging that children do need to access a level of risk. During this time, there was increasing awareness among researchers, educators and policy-makers about the importance of play in child development and, by the 1990s, many felt that overly safe playgrounds didn't provide children with sufficient opportunities for physical and cognitive development (Gill, 2007).

In 2012, the Health and Safety Executive (HSE) called for a balanced approach, stating that there was widespread misunderstanding of the legal requirements and that the goal should not be to remove all elements of risk: 'Play is great for children's well-being and development. When planning and providing play opportunities, the goal is not to eliminate risk, but to weigh up the risks and benefits. No child will learn about risk if they are wrapped in cotton wool' (HSE, 2012).

Case study: Becky, Rebecca and Mindy of *Thriving Language*

The natural outdoor environment provides the perfect springboard for children to engage in appropriate risky play. Risky play has an element of thrill, fear and excitement; knowing that there is the possibility of making a mistake, the possibility of harm and not knowing the outcome, adds to the pleasure of taking part. There is a growing body of evidence showing the importance of this type of play in childhood. Children learn to assess risks for themselves and deal with risks in the real world, both of which are important life skills. Trusting children means allowing them to direct their play and follow their internal drive to meet their own learning needs; not only will they be highly motivated, but also they will push their own boundaries of learning and create their own problems to solve – which will be at the edge of their zone of proximal development, providing opportunities for the most effective learning to take place. This is especially important when providing opportunities for appropriate risky play.

The educator's role is to observe and assess the child's skills, tune into the child's needs and respond to support and guide when needed. They are ultimately responsible for ensuring not only that the child is given these opportunities to learn through their own experiences, but also to support when, through dynamic risk assessment, they need to ensure the child's safety.

Reflective question 2.4

What are some strategies we can employ to create a balanced environment that ensures safety while also promoting healthy risk-taking?

Key takeaways

- Risk in play has always been an essential aspect of human development
- How we perceive play has changed and evolved over the years
- Sandseter's categories of risky play can be useful in terms of highlighting themes and patterns

(Continued)

- Early childhood theorists such as Froebel and Montessori advocated for risk in play
- Contemporary theorists state that risk in play is still important for survival
- Risky play has evolved to help children tackle normal phobias
- The HSE calls for a balanced approach. It wants practitioners to weigh up the risks and benefits

3

Why does it matter?

This is the place I like playing in. Here. It's hidden. They can't see me.

Stella, 4

This chapter

- Productive uncertainty (enabling children to engage with challenges)
- Risk deficit disorder which can lead to developmental issues
- Building resilience, enabling children to handle uncertainty and adapt to challenges in later life
- Barriers to risk in play such as climate change and urbanisation

Figure 3.1 Children need to access challenging environments

Productive uncertainty

I have coined the phrase 'productive uncertainty', borrowing this term from my husband, who's a financial advisor. I'm not sure I could explain what it means for those working in the financial sector, but, in play terms, I see it as children having access to an outdoor play environment where they can select challenges that are engaging and instructive (in the broadest sense). Outdoor play tends to be more unpredictable than indoor play.

A few years ago, I was asked to teach in higher education, a sector that was totally new to me. I tend to tell myself to approach these tasks 'one step at a time' to instil inner calm and I draw on my experience as a child, breaking down challenges such as riding my bike to 'just master this bit … then the next bit …'. I spend much of my day-to-day life outside with children and it's fascinating to see the way that each child will select the challenge they need. One child may feel a huge sense of accomplishment at touching mud whereas another wants to climb even higher than before.

The *just right challenge*, or *adaptive challenge*, devised by occupational therapist and psychologist Jean Ayres in the 1950s is central to my practice: providing activities and experiences that are appropriately challenging for each child. Rather than a level of challenge that is too overwhelming or too easy, the aim is to create the conditions for a just right level of challenge. Child development is not linear and the just right challenge ensures that each child is in that zone between boredom and frustration.

If you are reading this book, you are evidently thoughtful about the opportunities available to the children you work with. Unfortunately, some outdoor environments for children don't offer enough potential for productive uncertainty. Sterile, manicured spaces dominated by fake grass and fixed structures can limit children's creativity and development. Is the space inviting to children or just attractive to adults? As we will explain later on in the book, a huge space with expensive resources is not required.

There can be barriers to enabling children to move out of their comfort zone in play and start to challenge themselves physically and mentally. Below, we'll outline some of those barriers.

Reflective questions 3.1

Consider an outdoor space you are familiar with.

Does the space offer a just right challenge to children? How could it be improved?

Case study: Ellie Hodgkinson, lead practitioner at Lady Margaret Primary School

Our setting has very high numbers of children in the early stages of language acquisition; also, because of where we are in London and economic circumstances, children who come to us often really haven't had many experiences of anything at all beyond the family home/group. Many will have never been to the park for a variety of reasons.

So for children in our setting, risk begins with leaving parents on that first day, exploring a new space, communicating with adults who don't speak their home language, trying food they may have never seen before, playing with unknown children – let alone feeding the chickens, walking across the road to Forest School etc. That's why for us it's so important that we get those first few weeks right; we offer support and care and a gradual exposure to different types of experiences and the children learn that it's OK to take a risk, because they know that inherently it's a safe space where if something does go wrong there are trusted adults who can help if needed. We also need to work with parents to educate them about risk as many of our parents are completely risk-averse.

Risk deficit disorder

> *At school, we can't play Bulldogs, football is banned cuz they said it got too rough, we can't climb trees. The place where I live, there's a sign: 'no ball games'. My flat doesn't have a garden, there's just this bit of grass but you can't play ball games.*
>
> Sam, 8

As a young child in the 1970s, I often played outside without supervision, climbed trees (and occasionally fell out of them), used tools, cycled at great speed down steep hills and made wild dens. The world of children's play has changed a great deal since I was a child. Professor David Eager and Dr Helen Little have coined the term 'risk deficit disorder' to describe the context of modern play. They talk of 'the growing and unhealthy trend of attempting to remove all risk from within our community and the problems that this risk removal indirectly creates' (Eager and Little, 2011, p. 3). They believe that risk deficit disorder can lead to obesity, mental health issues, a lack of independence and a decrease in learning, perception and judgement skills.

At the Parks and Leisure Australia National Conference in 2011, Eager and Little emphasised that children are naturally drawn to play with risk. They desperately want to find out things for themselves, experiment and test their abilities. Eager and Little discuss the danger of creating a society of risk-averse citizens who have difficulties coping with situations with a normal level of challenge: risk in play is about engaging with and training for uncertainty. As adults, we face risk every day; Eager and Little believe that by making things too safe, children miss vital opportunities to learn about their physical and social world and their own capabilities. It can also drive children to find more dangerous locations to challenge themselves.

David Eager is Professor of Risk Management and Injury Prevention; in his opinion, many existing playgrounds are dull and uninspiring – playground designers need to consider opportunities for positive risk to ensure good outcomes for children. Eager suggests replacing the risk-averse mindset with a mindset that embraces the benefits of risk. Humans increasingly need the ability to tackle challenges and adjust in the face of changing situations, and these skills will become even more crucial as we face climate change emergencies.

Resilience doesn't prevent difficulties from happening in life, but it can make them easier to cope with. Studies show, on the one hand, that resilient children tend to be competent and more positive about themselves and life in general (Souri and Hasanirad, 2011). Adults with low levels of resilience, on the other hand, are more likely to resort to unhealthy and destructive coping mechanisms.

Climate change

We need to save the earth because we need nature.

Ella, 8

As well as resilient children, we now need to develop more resilient play spaces to take account of our rising temperatures, increased drought and more frequent flooding. I've had to change plans to cook over the fire with groups due to long periods of dry hot weather and warnings about increased fire risk. Heatwaves are making outdoor play more uncomfortable for young children in the UK at times. There has been an increase in extreme weather events, and I have had to cancel more and more outdoor sessions due to high winds. Water play can be a key part of risk in play, but water is a scarce commodity now in some areas whereas other areas struggle with flooding. The quality of water in our rivers and lakes is at an all-time low and this impacts on swimming or playing in rivers or lakes. Climate change has also had an effect on plant and animal species, so children won't be able to spot as many minibeasts and birds outdoors any more.

Ella Kissi-Debrah was a young girl who lived in London and tragically passed away in 2013 at the age of nine. Her death was initially attributed to acute respiratory failure and severe asthma. However, in 2018, a groundbreaking legal ruling in the UK concluded that air pollution, specifically traffic-related pollutants, contributed to her death. Poor air quality is already restricting children's outdoor activities, particularly for those with respiratory conditions.

Reflective questions 3.2

Are there any instances in your own practice where you have had to change plans or strategies due to sustainability concerns? How did you address these concerns?

What are some ways you might be able to address sustainability within your setting?

Urbanisation

I'm happy when I'm outside. I'm good at running and kicking, kicking the football and climbing, I'm good at climbing. When I go back from school, I'm indoors. I can't go out because J (kinship carer) has a new baby. I'm stuck … stuck in the house with the little ones.

Tom, 7 (not real name)

Increasing urbanisation in the UK has had an impact on outdoor play. As urban areas have become more densely populated, there are fewer green spaces for play, limiting opportunities for unstructured outdoor play in nature. This is what renowned author Richard Louv has labelled *nature deficit disorder*, where modern lifestyles, characterised by increased screen time, urbanisation and a decrease in outdoor activities, contribute to a lack of connection with the natural world.

Writer Tim Gill has raised concerns about the impact of increased urbanisation on outdoor play and he calls for urban environments that prioritise the well-being and play needs of children. Gill wants to see suitable spaces for children to enjoy physical activity, exploration and social interaction outdoors. Many community groups in the UK and beyond are working to address the so-called *play gap*, creating or reclaiming spaces for children's play. For example, Playing Out is a parent- and resident-led movement that reclaims streets for children's play: neighbours come together to organise and temporarily close their residential streets to traffic for a few hours. Children can then play freely, ride bikes and play physically without worrying about traffic hazards. The scheme has been successful, but it's not been without its detractors. As stated in the *Guardian* newspaper, some of the organisers of low traffic sessions have been threatened or even attacked (Wall, 2020).

Figure 3.2 Natural environments are at risk

Over protection

It's worth considering the language we use for staff. If they are called playground supervisors, they are going to be supervising. If they are called playground facilitators, they will facilitate play.

Felicity Robinson, Landscape Architect.

Over-sheltering children from all risks and micromanaging their lives can limit their opportunities to challenge themselves in play. For example, always stepping in to resolve conflicts or challenges denies children the chance to develop vital problem-solving and conflict resolution skills. We do need to risk assess, but overprotection can prevent children from exploring, taking risks, making decisions and choices, and experiencing failure. This can reduce children's opportunities to develop resilience and the ability to adapt.

David Ball, Professor of Risk Management, calls for balance, arguing that an overly risk-averse approach can deprive children of valuable learning experiences. Ball argues (Little and Eager, 2010) that an excessively cautious approach can hinder children's ability to learn how to navigate challenges and make decisions. He suggests that society tends to overestimate the dangers associated with certain activities and states that some level of risk is a normal part of childhood. Understanding and managing this risk is essential for healthy development.

Reflective questions 3.3

How has outdoor play changed since you were a child?

In your view, has the widespread use of social media by parents and carers affected children's access to risk in play? In what ways?

Lack of confidence of adults

If somebody feels unconfident about risk in play they are unlikely to encourage it and this lack of confidence can contribute to a more controlled and risk-averse educational environment. Children often take their cues from adults about how to approach new experiences and they can internalise anxious attitudes and become more risk-averse. This lack of confidence can be rooted in a range of factors, including limited experience of unstructured play. It can also come from untenable pressure from management and an overly high level of accountability. If practitioners work in a setting that does not support informed risk-taking, they can begin to doubt their understanding of child development. It's crucial that parents and careers are involved in the dialogue to avoid misunderstanding.

I find that there are specific areas such as climbing, tool use and rough-and-tumble play which can cause anxiety. Practitioners can worry about how to manage activities such as woodwork, for example. There is more guidance on this later in the book.

Fear of liability

There is sometimes significant pressure to use an overcautious approach or provide written documentation for every decision. This may lead to disproportionate procedures that undermine good judgement and leave children worse off, often indoors (Gill et al., 2019).

In our research for this book, a parent got in touch to tell us that play with sticks was banned in her child's playground and that children would have a stick taken off them if they were seen with one. Concerns about safety, liability and pressure to adhere to curriculum requirements have contributed to a more risk-averse culture in some educational settings. Staff may feel constrained in providing opportunities for risk in play due to fears of accidents, injuries, or potential backlash from parents or carers. In some settings, outdoor play has become overly structured and closely supervised due to fears of liability. Adults are playing a more active role in organising and overseeing activities and the environments are more adult-controlled. Practitioners can be put off by increased paperwork requirements and different policies that need to be written and maintained. (Working in Early Years during the lockdowns, I was almost overwhelmed by the ever-changing requirements of the government paperwork.)

However, in recent years, there's been a growing recognition of the importance of risk and the value of benefit–risk assessments where educators evaluate the potential benefits of an activity against the risks involved. In most settings staff encourage a nuanced approach to risk management that allows for healthy challenges while ensuring safety. We will explore this in more detail later in the book.

Reflective question 3.4

Research shows that we all have subconscious bias around risk.

How could you try to ensure that your health and safety policies represent different viewpoints?

Decreased outdoor playtime

Children today tend to spend less time playing outdoors compared to previous generations. Increased academic pressures, structured schedules and the rise of indoor entertainment, including gaming and streaming services, have contributed to a decline in outdoor play. A study by University College London (UCL) found that school break times have decreased significantly over the past two decades, leading to children missing out on valuable opportunities for social interaction, physical exercise and free time.

The study compared data from over 1,000 primary and secondary schools. It revealed that children at Key Stage 1 have 45 minutes less break time per week compared to 1995, and Key Stage 3 and 4 pupils have 65 minutes less. There has been an almost virtual elimination of afternoon breaks, with only 15 per cent of Key Stage 2 children and just over half of Key Stage 1 children having an afternoon break. In 1995, 13 per cent of secondary schools reported an afternoon break period, compared to only 1 per cent now. Lunch breaks have also been cut down, with 82 per cent of secondary schools reporting lunch breaks of less than 55 minutes. A quarter of secondary schools have lunchtimes of 35 minutes or less. Almost 60 per cent of schools withhold breaks from children as a consequence of poor behaviour or incomplete work (Baines and Blatchford, 2023). The researchers suggest that the reduction in break times could have serious implications for children's well-being and development and have found that children are now half as likely to meet up with friends outside school.

Sedentary lifestyles

I run and I run and I run, fall on the grass, and roll down!

Jed, 4

Angela Hanscom, an occupational therapist based in the US, became increasingly concerned about the dangers of limiting unstructured play. She went on to found TimberNook, an outdoor play-based programme designed to encourage children's creativity and independent play. Hanscom believes that modern society tends to overprotect children, leading to a lack of opportunities for them to engage in activities that involve risk, challenge and problem-solving. According to Hanscom, these experiences are crucial for the development of physical, emotional and cognitive skills. Through activities like climbing trees, balancing on uneven surfaces, or engaging in other physically challenging activities, children learn to develop their proprioception (awareness of their body in space), problem solving skills and self regulation.

Studies indicate that less time outdoors is causing higher levels of short-sightedness. Following one of the largest studies of its kind, it was established that more than one in three children and young people are shortsighted, prompting calls for less screen time and more physical activity. There has been a dramatic increase in myopia over the last 30 years (Gregory, 2024). Hanscom suggests that exposing children to manageable risks during play also helps them develop essential life skills and face challenges in the future. She argues that well-intentioned but overly protective parenting and constantly shuttling children between different activities can limit a child's opportunities for appropriately challenging play. A lack of physical activity and outdoor play can contribute to developmental issues and diminish a child's ability to assess and navigate risks.

Financial considerations

Schools and nurseries are working with reduced budgets; this has had an impact on outdoor play. For example, many settings are struggling to afford wet-weather clothing for children and staff. Outdoor space is also at a premium. A lack of funding can lead to a shortage of staff, which can mean that educators are hesitant to allow risky play. When teaching in Reception, I often did not have a TA in class with me. Insufficient resources can also limit staff training so that staff feel less confident about enabling play that has an element of risk.

Reflective question 3.5

Consider your own setting. What might be some barriers to risk in play in your setting?

Key takeaways

- Providing opportunities for productive uncertainty in outdoor play is crucial for healthy child development
- Encouraging risk in play helps children learn essential life skills, including resilience and problem-solving
- Climate change and urbanisation are creating barriers to outdoor play, making it essential to develop resilient play spaces
- We need to balance safety and learning to avoid overprotection, which can limit children's opportunities to grow and challenge themselves
- Supportive environments – both physical and social – are necessary to foster a child's natural curiosity and risk-taking in play

4

The benefits of risky play

The more risks you allow children to take, the better they learn to take care of themselves. If you never let them take any risks, then I believe they become very prone to injury.

Dahl, 1993

This chapter

- How we encounter risk throughout life
- Risk we encounter in physical development
- Benefits of free play
- Supporting behaviour through providing risk and challenge
- Other documentation that supports practitioners to facilitate risk in play

Risk as part of development

Babies (let's assume we are talking about the first year of a child's life), when it comes to risk, are probably the easiest to manage. What I mean by that is that it is the only stage of a child's development where we, as the adults, have all the control. It's on us as primary caregivers – parents or practitioners – if they roll off the bed or changing table when we turn our backs or pick up a 'dangerous' object. So, we baby-proof our environments and move choking hazards and sharp things out of reach. We make things safe. As adults we have carried out a risk assessment and nothing is left to chance.

Then, somewhere generally between six months to about two years old, everything changes. Babies become toddlers and develop increasing curiosities and physical abilities. As adults we encourage this, of course. Whether parent or practitioner, we encourage and celebrate all these new 'firsts' – rolling over, crawling, first solid foods, communication, mark-making, pulling themselves up against furniture, first steps with a walker, first steps unaided, then riding their bike/trike, jumping … then woah! we want to put the brakes on. Our language becomes limiting. 'Walk don't run! Don't jump from there, it's too high! Don't ride so fast! Use your brakes!' It all gets a little scary (for the adults that is). For many children there is no fear, only wonder, curiosity and excitement to learn yet more amazing new skills. 'Look at me!'

Of course, when we are in a caregiving role, we want to keep our charges as safe as possible. But in keeping them safe from exposure to any risk are we actually doing children a disservice? Knowing, as we do, about child development, we know this to be true. However, in practice, it can be an uncomfortable truth. How do we come to terms with actively exposing children to risk? Is that in fact what we are doing? Increasingly, the language around this is changing – from an expectation that children always be kept 'as safe as possible' to 'as safe as necessary'. And here we can really start to unpick the benefits of play with an element of risk.

If we support and encourage the possibility for children to explore their own physical competency (for example), then there is growing evidence that highlights all the ways in which children benefit. In a managed space which is 'as safe as necessary', but which provides for active, challenging play, we are creating a safety net of sorts where children can learn and understand about their own competence (and limitations), challenge themselves, learn autonomy, independence, responsibility (for their choices and decisions – and feel empowered to make those decisions), perseverance, mastery.

> Children want and need to take risks when they play. Play provision aims to respond to these needs and wishes by offering children stimulating, challenging environments for exploring and developing their abilities. In doing this, play provision aims to manage the level of risk so that children are not exposed to unacceptable risks of death or serious injury.
>
> Play Safety Forum, 2008, p. 1

David Ball (2007), mentioned previously, supports this in his statement that 'children need to learn somewhere about the reality of risk and the reality of the consequences of occasionally falling foul of it' (p. 68). Children need to have opportunities to make decisions about what type of play to engage in and how far they want to challenge themselves. They also need to be given the time to make these decisions without feeling rushed, as that is when we veer into unnecessary risk territory: 'Every setting needs to consider the balance between safety and a decent level of challenge in physical play, as well as exciting activities that stretch children intellectually and emotionally' (Lindon, 1999, p. 47).

Free play

An indoor environment can provide a tremendous range of options for babies and very young children to explore risk, but, as children grow, they occupy more space and consequently need a wider range of opportunities in order to be challenged and to grow, in every sense of the word. Scientific and anecdotal research has taught us that issues such as boredom, anxiety, difficulty with attention span and focus, everyday frustrations and even aggression are frequently due, at least in part, to a lack of opportunities to develop gross motor skills and engage in a variety of sensory experiences in the Early Years (and throughout childhood). Angela Hanscom states:

> Active free play outdoors is a kind of play that promotes healthy sensory and motor development in children. The outdoors awakens and rejuvenates the mind and engages all the senses at once. In nature children learn to take risks, overcome fears, make new friends, regulate emotions, and create imaginary worlds.
>
> Hanscom, 2016, p. 3

A broad range of physical play options challenges the vestibular system, develops core strength and gross motor skills. Specific activities that in years gone by have been an exclusively grown-up domain can additionally develop fine motor skills (thinking specifically here about the use of tools and fire in Early Years). If we can demystify these traditionally 'adult' pastimes that otherwise can develop into fascination to explore without adults' support, we may even be able to reduce incidents and accidents and, dare I say, wilful and deliberate acts such as arson.

Play strategy across the UK

Play is listed as one of the key features of the Early Years Collaborative. Scotland's play strategy has undergone recent updates, both pre-Covid and another looking at the impacts of Covid. Play Scotland now also has a play charter, and a wealth of other play resources released in recent years, such as the Loose Parts toolkit, the Free to Play guide and the Parents Play Pack (all available at playscotland.org). The *Play Map* (Elsley, 2015) identifies very clearly the priorities as linked to Article 31, and links to the specific responsibilities of those with the power to make a difference, as well as to other resources which should be considered. For example, 'Action 1: Uphold principles underpinning a commitment to play' in the *Play Map* states:

> CPPs [Community Planning Partnerships] take account of the benefits as well as the risks of play.

Figure 4.1 Tool use in an Early Years setting

> How does the CPP ensure that its responsibilities in relation to risk are proportionate to the benefits of play?
>
> Does the CPP incorporate child-friendly community assessment processes and indicators into its existing practice?
>
> p. 10

Play England introduced its first play strategy in 2008, but despite featuring planning as far as 2020 it was aborted by the then government only two years in. Play England is undertaking what is has termed a re-'imagineering' (coming from 'imagination' and 'engineering', which is the implementation of creative ideas in practical form) of its organisational work during 2024 (Play England, n.d.b). At the heart of this is a new ten-year strategy and call on the current government to introduce play sufficiency legislation. This is closely aligned with Wales, who were the first of the UK nations to introduce statutory legislation around play with their play sufficiency legislation. PlayBoard Northern Ireland (PlayBoard NI, 2024) has been involved in moving forward play policy for a good decade, and is currently working to a three-year strategy plan.

It is heartening that there is so much work being done across the UK on play strategy and play sufficiency, and that all four nations are represented on the International Play Association World Council of 20 member countries (International Play Association, n.d.b). The buzz from the IPA World Conference held in Glasgow in 2024 does appear to have had a significant effect on the continuing movement to embed play not only in culture, but also in strategy for all of our children. We can all support this by having in place our own play charter or strategy for our organisation. In some areas this is already supported by a local authority play strategy, and so on. Outdoor Play and Learning (OPAL) (n.d.) has been working in primary schools to support the play offer that we see in Early Years to continue throughout the primary years. As part of the programme schools are encouraged to develop their own play charter. OPAL has just sponsored the launch of the 'Plan for Play' in Parliament, a joint statement calling on all parties to insist schools have a plan for the 20 per cent of their school day that is playtime.

Reflective question 4.1

Consider your own setting.

What might be some key points you think should be in your play charter?

So, the pressure is on to keep play high on the agenda. Play can be best facilitated by providing a space for children where they can feel safe and protected yet have the potential to explore and take risks. This can look very different in different settings and may range from a playground with a variety of loose parts to a larger expanse of park or woodland. Ideally there will be a variety of opportunities to move and play in different ways, so that children are able to engage in all of the different play types. The ideal environment will provide places to hide as well as open space, obstacles and challenges. Space to run, climb and jump or to build and create. Children can be allowed to play uninterrupted though still with a sense of attachment to the adults around, who will model availability and interest without control.

If we have the opportunity to use a local green space or woodland for play, or possibly even when considering the existing grounds of our school or Early Years setting, we need to consider many factors such as who else uses the area? Are there clear boundaries? How does the area change with different seasons/weather? Is there a range of trees, undergrowth and terrain for different types of play? What features can we maximise for play? Do any features offer more in risk than they do in benefit? What can we change so that we can make the most of the space while causing minimal impact to the natural environment? One of the benefits of play in a natural environment is the way it connects the children (and adults) with the space.

Reflective questions 4.2

Consider an outdoor space you are familiar with. What factors can you think of that might need to be considered?

What are some risky play benefits the space offers?

What are some risks that need to be assessed?

Observations at a fully outdoor setting highlight that physical or locomotor play is most common, with tree climbing, see-saw balancing, jumping, swinging, running and sliding happening all the time and something most children can be seen engaged in during most sessions. Much of this type of play involves 'look at me' development and celebration of achievements, often repeating or copying something achieved by one of their peers. There is healthy and positive respect for one another's abilities and a collaborative support network to help each other to achieve the skill.

Figure 4.2 Collaborative play and supporting each other

From barriers to benefits

Play actively engages children in the world around them, enhancing their cognitive, communication, physical and social/emotional development. Play is a child's right (UNCRC: UN, 1989) and the gateway to learning – all learning comes from play. As we've touched on already, the main barrier that can get in the way of free play tends to be the adults! If the session is prescriptive with activities pre-planned and directed, then it is not free play. Even with no resources, children will make their own play – providing *open-ended* resources can enhance the type and quality of the play, but *closed* resources with no room for imagination and creativity can also create barriers by limiting or stifling the opportunities for play. Health and safety can be a barrier to free play where the adults are risk-averse and unable to assess the activities with a benefit–risk approach. Adults' fear of the 'what if …?' can be limiting.

Adults need to understand what free play is and the best way to grasp this is to observe a session where free play is taking place – to realise that children don't need micro-managing and directing in their play, that they can be trusted to make choices and direct their own activities. Once this is happening, the adults can then allow the children space and time to play, standing back yet not detached from the activity, assessing how and when (or if) to interject. Loose parts can be provided very simply and cheaply, mostly for free in the form of pallets, cardboard boxes, plastic pipes/tubing, planks and offcuts of wood, tyres. Chapter 8 will discuss the use of loose parts, which along with other benefits encourage children to engage in hard physical work – something else that sometimes we can shy away from supporting as adults.

> The forest school experience provides an environment where children can develop confidence and competence. As Froebel discovered: 'they do not want the easy occupations, but the hard work which demands strength and exertion'.
>
> Lilley, 1967, cited in Bruce, 2012, p. 66

This view is further supported by Benjamin Spock, an American paediatrician who said: 'a child loves his play not because it's easy but because it's hard' (1946, p. 404). A detailed benefit–risk assessment allows all adults to see the benefits listed as well as to be reassured that the potential for risk has been considered and the level of risk assessed and managed. Time spent with children teaches adults that they are capable and can be trusted to assess their own risk.

> The more children are free to engage in risky play the better they will be at managing risks, judging what they are capable of, and keeping themselves safe. The role of the teacher is to provide a challenging and risky learning environment that will support all children as they become more motivated, curious, able, and adventurous.
>
> Outdoor Risky Play for All, blog post 2013

Supporting behaviour

Evidence in practice also shows us that children's behaviour can be significantly impacted by the opportunity to play in a very physical and challenging way. Children's achievements in terms of overcoming physical challenge; in creative challenges like using tools to change or build/make something; being the one who is able to light the fire demonstrate the capacity of the child to 'get it right' when provided with the resources and scaffolding to do so. We are promoting the idea of focusing on their intrinsic motivation. Behaviour can be significantly impacted by self-esteem – not only by low self-esteem, but also by an over-inflated sense of self-worth. Both scenarios can come from lack of opportunities to undertake tasks for oneself or to take risks rather than having everything done by others. Risky play and challenging tasks in particular can have a positive impact on a child's developing self-esteem. When we share these outcomes with parents and they begin to see their child as capable, the child's whole world can shift.

Self-determination theory (often simply referred to in education as SDT) suggests that learners have a natural tendency to explore their environments, to grow, learn and develop. In order to fully maximise the opportunities provided and remain motivated to progress, they also need to feel autonomy, competence and a sense of belonging. The wider the community of support, the potentially greater the impact. 'Parents need to be part of a learning community in which together with the practitioners who spend time with their children they develop their understanding about what makes the best practise in developing children to flourish' (Bruce, 2012, p. 27).

The ethos of Forest School is based on a fundamental respect for children and young people and for their capacity to instigate, test and maintain curiosity in the world around them. It believes in children's right to play; the right to access the outdoors (in particular a woodland environment); the right to access risk and the vibrant reality of the natural world; and the right to experience a healthy range of emotions, through all the challenges of social interaction, to build a resilience that will enable continued and creative engagement with their peers and their potential (FSTC, n.d.).

Facing our fears

The words 'what if …?' are so often preceded by a 'but' and prompted by fear and expectation of negative outcomes. What if we can focus on reframing that so every 'what if …?' is an opportunity for positivity, for growth, for learning and discovering?

> 'Supposing a tree fell down, Pooh, when we were underneath it?'
>
> 'Supposing it didn't!' said Pooh after careful thought.
>
> Piglet was comforted by this.
>
> Milne and Shepard, 1928, p. 132

Reflective questions 4.3

What are some of your own 'what if ...?'s?

Are there any particular elements of your professional practice that cause fear for you?

Can you think of any strategies you currently use or could use in future to reframe that fear?

As adults, we can rationalise that a way of overcoming a fear is to face that fear, to experience it and then, frequently, the fear reduces. We may not achieve a goal at the first attempt, but by persevering at something we find hard, the sense of achievement when we finally get it is far greater than if it had come easily to us in the first place. As educators, we know the importance of failure and making mistakes to ultimately learning a skill or developing knowledge. We don't expect perfection on the first attempt (if ever!). Trying again (and again) is an important part of the process. So it is with risk in play – by providing such opportunities we are providing significant potential for learning. Through exposure to controlled risk-taking and feelings of fear, such as those experienced through play, children learn to cope with and overcome fear and anxiety. This strengthens their ability to cope when faced with situations which invoke similar feelings in other contexts, thus contributing hugely to resilience and overall mental well-being. Furthermore, when engaging in play with risk, children are developing additional skills such as problem-solving. It can even support language development, as children find ways of expressing their feelings or relating their experiences, of supporting each other or asking for help. For further reading around this, you may wish to look at the work of Helen Dodd (Dodd and Lester, 2021) and Gladstone and Rice (2016).

Case study: social responsibility

Eleanor Bernardes is an education leadership researcher and consultant and a PhD candidate

We've just moved from Naples to Norway. Everything is risky in Naples. Houses aren't built properly, and bits of my house would routinely just fall off because there weren't building regulations. We lived on a dual carriageway with no pavement, so you'd walk the kids at the side of it to go to school in

(Continued)

the morning. You always felt like you were looking out for disaster. You never felt safe. Everything was always a threat, so we spent three years being in a heightened sense of threat awareness and our kids thought that was normal. But, at the same time, Italian parenting is really to wrap your children in cotton wool.

When we moved to Scandinavia, within the first day of arriving, we saw three-year-olds walking to school on their own. My children took a couple of weeks to adjust, but have now just thrived. They can go to the park or walk to school on their own. Things are safer and people feel that if something did go wrong, other people would be there to look out for their children. The environment has been created to be safe and the children should be allowed to take those risks.

Norway has a sense of social responsibility. This is a country that invests very heavily in police and infrastructure and cycle paths and lighting. In Norway it feels like the state has said 'we want people to be independent, so we're going create as secure an environment as possible and then you can let your child do whatever they want to'.

In Stavanger, one of the things it is famous for is this outcrop called Pulpit Rock. There are no handrails. The cruise ships come into Stavanger, and they unload all these people who've been on a cruise for a week and take them on a massive hike. It's not easy and you see people doing it in flip flops. But people recognise this is a dangerous activity and that they need to take responsibility for themselves. You're not lulled into a sense of security by a handrail.

Key takeaways

- Risk is an intrinsic, essential part of child development
- We should keep children 'as safe as necessary' rather than 'as safe as possible'
- Children need a range of opportunities including those involving risk to learn and grow
- We can use the features of our environment to support and maximise opportunities for play
- Children need 'hard work' and challenge

5
The rights of the child

A person's a person, no matter how small.

Dr Seuss, 1954

This chapter

- What the UNCRC is and what it means in different parts of the UK
- Article 31 and its relevance
- What this means for risk and play

The UNCRC

The United Nations Convention on the Rights of the Child (UN, 1989) is a legally binding international agreement (ratified by every country in the world except the US at the time of writing) – setting out the civil, political, economic, social and cultural rights of every child, regardless of their race, religion or abilities. It is an international agreement which protects the human rights of children up to the age of 18, even if their country has not signed the Universal Declaration on Human Rights. It recognises not only their basic human rights, but also gives them additional rights to protect them from harm as one of the most vulnerable groups in society. It is the most ratified international human rights treaty in history, and was ratified in the UK in 1991; however, it is worth keeping in mind that ratification alone does not guarantee fulfilment of all aspects unless it is incorporated into domestic law in that country.

The UNCRC is made up of 54 'articles' or statements, which cover different aspects of a child's life and include civil, political, economic, social and cultural rights. One of these articles – Article 31 – refers specifically to children's right to play, and it is this article that everyone working with children in any capacity should be guided by when it comes to providing opportunities for children to play. Article 31 states that:

> 1. [...] Parties recognize the right of the child to rest and leisure, to engage in play and recreational activities appropriate to the age of the child and to participate freely in cultural life and the arts.
>
> 2. [...] Parties shall respect and promote the right of the child to participate fully in cultural and artistic life and shall encourage the provision of appropriate and equal opportunities for cultural, artistic, recreational and leisure activity.
>
> UN, 1989

In 2013 the United Nations Committee on the Rights of the Child adopted General Comment No. 17 that emphasises for governments across the world the meaning and importance of Article 31 (Play England, n.d.a).

Reflective questions 5.1

Consider your own setting.

Are there practices currently in place that support the principles laid out in Article 31?

How could these practices be expanded on or improved?

For anyone who would like to look further into this subject, the International Play Association's (IPA, 2013) video *This Is Me: Article 31 and a Child's Right to Play* is a fantastic resource that defies anyone with a beating heart not to smile and feel uplifted by the many different ways in which children across the world play. Play is a true leveller, where we can see that there is more that unites us than divides us. As half of the authorship of this book, I am proud to live in Scotland where, on 16 January 2024, children's right to play was incorporated into Scots law (Scottish Parliament, 2024). The United Nations Convention on the Rights of the Child (Incorporation) (Scotland) Act incorporates the UNCRC (1989) into the law in Scotland. This makes Scotland the first country in the UK, and the first devolved nation in the world, to directly incorporate the UNCRC into domestic law. Wales has also been a world leader in its commitment to upholding the UNCRC and to play, being the first country in the world to establish duties around play provision into its legislation in 2014, having formally adopted the UNCRC in 2004. One could be forgiven for seeing this as slow progress, but, depending on your historical and/or world lens, there have been dramatic developments in our lifetime that our parents (or grandparents certainly) could not have imagined.

For anybody not totally familiar with the UNCRC it might be described as a kind of treasure map, magnificently outlining the rights of every child worldwide. Adopted by the United Nations General Assembly in 1989, this visionary document identifies four key principles: non-discrimination; the best interests of the child; the right to life, survival and development; and the right to be heard. Within this labyrinth of rights, lies the often-underestimated right to play and explore. Play is a fundamental right. Childhood without play is like a rainbow without colours, rather dull and unrecognisable. What is often overlooked in children's play is their right to choose their activities and, yes, even choose risky activities. Committed, passionate and creative teachers and Early Years professionals spend hours of their time planning beautiful sessions for the children in their care. Initial teacher education still has a huge focus on planning, and educational practitioners are expected to demonstrate a range of creative ideas, to plan activities that will meet a range of educational outcomes and cover every aspect of the broad curriculum. However, those who direct us to plan in this way risk ignoring the capability of children to design their own activities, to take themselves on a learning journey and to successfully navigate all aspects of the curriculum without a large amount of interference from the adults around them. The 2013 General Comment No. 17 states:

> Children benefit from recreational activities involving adults, including voluntary participation in organized sports, games and other recreational activities. However, the benefits are diminished, particularly in the development of creativity, leadership and team spirit if control by adults is so pervasive that it undermines the child's own efforts to organize and conduct his or her play activities.
>
> UN Committee on the Rights of the Child, 2013

The UNCRC recognises that play is crucial for children's physical mental and social development. Play is a magical potion of imagination, creativity and social interaction. It is the secret ingredient that turns the mundane into the extraordinary for little adventurers. So far so good, I think we'd all agree, and the above description is one I'd guess most of us are happy with. Now let's throw a twist into the tale – children's right to choose risky activities. Yes, the UNCRC acknowledges that children have the right to take risks, explore uncertainties and challenge their boundaries. That doesn't mean we have to turn every environment into an adventure park, but rather that we should give consideration to creating environments where controlled risk-taking is as welcome as a rainbow after the rain. As educators we often find ourselves torn between safety and adventure as if they are mutually exclusive; it's a delicate balancing act where risk is not the enemy but rather a partner in the creation of the ideal experience for all children. Children, much like adults, are active citizens with rights. As teachers and practitioners, our role is to guide them, not control them. Imagine a world where children actively participate in decisions that affect them, where their voices echo through the corridors of power. This is not just a dream; it's a reality outlined in the UNCRC, where children have the right to be heard and their opinions respected. So, why not let them have a say in their play?

Reflective questions 5.2

How do you feel when you see children climbing trees, building makeshift forts, or navigating obstacle courses?

What is your instinctive response?

Are there events in your own life that might influence the way you respond?

Consider your answers to the reflective questions. You might have answered with words like 'nervous' or 'unsettled'; however, we know that it's through such provocatively playful activities that children learn to assess risks, make decisions and develop resilience. The UNCRC doesn't shy away from encouraging these seemingly risky exploits. Instead, it invites us to view them as stepping stones towards holistic development.

Figure 5.1 Several children climbing a tree

General Comment No.17 also states that one of the factors for an optimum environment is:

> Space and opportunities to play outdoors unaccompanied in a diverse and challenging physical environment, with easy access to supportive adults, when necessary.
>
> (UN Committee on the Rights of the Child, 2013)

In a world dominated by the fear of recrimination and even litigation, safety concerns often cast a dark shadow over our playgrounds. But what if we burst that fear bubble and embraced the notion that children are more resilient and capable than we give them credit for? The UNCRC challenges us to create environments where children can stretch their limits, stumble and, yes, occasionally scrape their knees – a small price for the invaluable lessons learned.

As educators, our mission is not to eliminate all risks, but to empower children to navigate them. We are the navigators, the facilitators and the cheerleaders for their journey. By providing a safe space for controlled risks, we foster a sense of agency, independence and responsibility. The UNCRC (1989) is encouragingly behind us, urging us to be the wind beneath their wings rather than clipping them, reminding us that every child, regardless of ability, has the right to play and take risks. Every child bar none. Every child, with their unique sets of abilities, their individual spirits, ideas and visionary dreams, is master of their inclusive playground of rights.

Children, by nature, are rebels with a cause – the cause of exploring, questioning and challenging the norm. The UNCRC invites us to celebrate this spirit of playful rebellion, encouraging children to voice their opinions, challenge rules and actively participate in shaping their environment. So, why not let them be the architects of their play spaces, advocating for swings, slides, building materials and resources for them to let their imaginations run free and create the play that their minds dream of and also that their bodies need. Play, risk and empowerment go hand-in-hand, just as in the journey of education from the not-so-distant past to where learning now actively seeks to include fun and laughter. Every child matters and so do their ideas, their desires and their rights. Being the lead actor in one's own life should not be a feature reserved for adulthood; it should begin in childhood and in play.

Helping children to lead

> *[The] child is free to determine his own actions according to the laws and demands of the play he is involved in. Through and in his play he is able to feel himself to be independent and autonomous.*
>
> Froebel, in Liebschner, 1992, p. 69

Play is often dependent on adults who control the environment, the resources available, time allowed for play and also the type of play which is allowed. Tyrie et al. (2019) found that school staff often limited play through fears over the weather, value judgements about the types of play and insisting upon imposing rules or structure to play sessions. If children were able to have greater autonomy over such decision-making, we might see different decisions and different outcomes. Through the introduction of *freeflow* set-ups and indoor–outdoor settings, children have greater freedom to choose where to play – indoors or outdoors – regardless of weather. Penny Holland's (2003) book *We Don't Play with Guns Here* has helped us as adults to consider our own feelings about weapon play as an example of one type of play which has often been disallowed.

I had the privilege recently to witness a situation where a play facilitator had a no-balls rule outside a designated area. A group of boys negotiated to have the use of a ball to play a game in an area that they had determined could be safe for others, not intrude on others' play and they'd created some rules to ensure it could not become a problem. An agreement was reached, and the boys knew they risked losing their ball and their game if breached. They successfully governed their own play for the remainder of the term, proving that they could be trusted. Similarly, groups of under-fives have proved they can regulate turn-taking on a swing through the use of a sand-timer.

Reflective questions 5.3

Can you think of any experience you've had with children self-regulating, or negotiating like this?

How did you respond?

Case study: 'Can they climb up there?'

Kierna Corr is a Nursery Teacher at Windmill Integrated Primary School, Dungannon, County Tyrone

In 2008 I was fortunate to spend a week with an outdoor class in a kindergarten in Norway. I think for the first few days my mouth remained open the whole time as I constantly asked, 'Can they climb up there, should they be up there, are they allowed to do that/move that?' etc. The staff were very patient with me and my questions, but did eventually ask me to leave the children alone to play and step back! This is when I noticed that the staff were all quite hands off and weren't organising adult-led activities for the children, rather standing back and observing the play, only stepping in if and when needed. The mantra I heard that week was: 'If they can get up, they can get down.' Staff explained that children generally got stuck when adults lifted them up onto structures or into trees rather than allowing the children to self-evaluate the risk for themselves.

Roll on 15 years and if you visited our setting, you would see children climbing up on ladders, pallets and adult-sized picnic seats to look over the fence or in and out of wooden potato boxes, and they are allowed to move some of the wooden logs and tree stumps as long as they put them back when finished. It is usual in the first term to hear a child shout 'Help, I'm stuck!' but we don't simply lift them down or out. We talk to them about how they might climb out or down for themselves and are there to help them if they panic or get truly stuck, but the majority will manage to get themselves 'unstuck' with some encouragement. The sense of achievement they feel is always wonderful to witness.

Our day in nursery is now a much slower-paced one than it used to be, with very few transitions. The play can ebb and flow through the day as children are afforded long periods of time to truly 'wallow in play' as Tina Bruce discusses (2012). I am finding that there are fewer conflicts in the class. It is all about trust, the adults need to trust the children and see them as confident and capable learners; the families need to trust the staff to offer play opportunities with risk; and staff need to trust that they will not be blamed if children do fall or get hurt.

Key takeaways

- The UNCRC is ratified in the UK though not legally binding except in Scotland
- Article 31 of the UNCRC focuses on children's right to play
- The UNCRC – in particular, Article 31 – encourages us to facilitate a variety of play opportunities, including those with risk
- We can help children to exercise their rights

Part 2

Creating an environment for risky play

Having established what we mean by risky play and established the benefits and importance of access to activities and situations that provide elements of risk and challenge, what exactly is it that we are trying to facilitate and foster through provision of this nature in the Early Years? As Early Years teachers and practitioners, we are not only expected to provide a rationale for the experiences we provide, but we generally also enjoy and engage with this process of justification. We want other professionals and the families of the children we work with to 'get it' and to be as excited about this learning and development process as we are in providing it.

Throughout this section we are going to consider the outcomes that we want and expect children to achieve through exposure to risky play.

6

What are we trying to facilitate and foster?

If we are going to educate students with lifelong global learning in mind, it follows that students should develop the skills with which to manage the risks they will encounter throughout their lives.

Beames et al. (2024)

This chapter

- The importance of play in childhood
- Risky experiences in childhood contribute to overwhelmingly positive memories
- Risk as an important part of overall health and well-being
- The importance of experiencing challenge and developing competence

Making memories

There is another, non-academic and non-measured reason for promoting these adventurous opportunities for children. How often have you found yourself using the phrase 'making memories' when talking passionately about your work with these small humans that you care so deeply about? Memories are one of the greatest gifts we can give to our children, and it is these memories that will lead them to continue to seek out new experiences and find their own passions in life as they grow.

Play Wales have put together an excellent film called *This is Why Play is So Important* (2023). If you haven't seen it, it is recommended watching (we're not really here to make recommendations, but this is worth deviating from the brief a little for). The film features children of all ages, from pre-school to teen, and also adults, who reflect on their play memories. During the film you see lots of examples of things that could be referred to as risky play, again featuring children of all ages. The adults' stories are particularly impactful for a couple of reasons. Firstly, there is the uncontained joy in their faces and voices as they recall some of their standout play memories. Then there is the fact that the majority of the adult memories involve risk, with several also involving injury. But the outcomes resulting in injury are given very little reference, and the enduring emotion is one of joy – these are happy memories and speak of feelings of freedom and invincibility. The following quotes are from some of the contributors' stories in the film. These are adults, male and female, ranging in age from around 20s to 50s now, demonstrating that time has not diminished these significant times in their childhood.

> The first play memory I can remember, there was a swing in the park and me and my friend, I can't remember their name, but we used to swing and see how high and fast we could get and right at the top of the swing we jump off which is probably really dangerous, but it honestly felt like flying!
>
> I remember being so happy that we had this slide in our back garden; we thought it would be fun ('cause by then we've got tired of just going down in the normal way), just to climb to the top and jump off the side. Didn't end well … I ended up breaking both my wrists!
>
> … and we used to run across the flat roof and jump across the across the gap and we got really very, very good at it. So, we devised a game where we would set markers further and further away from the gap, and one fateful day I took a run at it with a marker that was probably four or five feet away from the edge and I didn't make the gap. So, I hit the other building and [it] felt like a really slow motion fall down the side of the building to the floor, and my overriding memory (apart from the fact that my trousers were in shreds and there was blood all down my legs) was looking back up at my mates who were absolutely killing themselves laughing!
>
> So, the first memory I've got is being out up the mountains, sometimes we'd come in over lunch, sometimes we didn't, but playing out with my friends all the time. There's a theme to my early play memories and that is that if I was outside there were no adults around and nobody had any idea where I was. It was, well it was freedom really.

Watching the film and seeing the people at the centre of these stories tell them with their own expressions really brings them to life.

Reflective questions 6.1

What risky activities featured in your childhood?

Have you noticed others – young or old – talking about risky play or adventurous activities in a positive way?

Health and risk

While anecdotal 'evidence' such as the memories of children-now-adults is hardly robust scientific data, children and their development is not only about the scientific data and education theory that we 'know' (using inverted commas because what we 'know' changes by generation; we are still learning so much). Children are complex, developing character and emotions, likes and dislikes, feelings and responses, resilience and competencies. The same lived experience will impact different people in different ways, however much we try to control the variables. Consider this anecdote based in evidence and accumulated data from a practising GP in Scotland: she stated that she sees more children with anxiety and mental health issues currently than she does children with broken bones or injuries from playing outside. These observations are replicated across the country and data is forming.

This echoes some of the work done by Mariana Brussoni and colleagues on collating data relating to injuries to children as a result of risky play. As an example, one study states that:

> fracture frequency and severity was not related to height of playground equipment. Ulna-radius fractures (most frequent type of fracture, accounting for 42% of playground fractures) were as likely to occur below 59" (54%) as they were above the mark (46%). The six reported tibia fractures occurred below 59". No fractures to the head or spine occurred as a result from a fall from playground equipment.
>
> Brussoni et al., 2015, p. 6441

It sounds cavalier to say that broken bones are not that big a deal. It is impossible to rule out the chance of severe injury. But the data continues to support that such catastrophic injuries are far more likely when crossing roads or travelling as a passenger in a car, rather than playing in woods or playgrounds.

In a podcast for the Association for Child and Adolescent Mental Health (ACAMH) Helen Dodd talks about *Adventurous Play: A Prevention for Anxiety* (2022). It is a statement, not a question. In the podcast Dodd talks about how her research has led her to be convinced that this link is direct and unequivocal. Before she began to pay attention to children's play, her research was all about the risk factors for anxiety – why do children develop anxieties? She began to think about this in the context of adventurous play and was able to connect that lots of the feelings related to anxiety can be targeted by the experience that children have when they play adventurously. That feeling of slight fear, anticipation, butterflies in the tummy, being on the edge of your comfort zone – we can feel a little nervous, even scared, but within a safe space these feelings can also be good feelings, something we look to repeat, through play. When we experience these feelings of fear in a positive context, we learn our coping mechanisms, and when the body has a similar response in a different context, we are more able to cope.

Figure 6.1 Children experiencing exciting movement play with a trusted caregiver

Children are also more likely to respond to challenging opportunities for play if this is modelled to them, by their peers or by the adults they are with, and they receive the message that its OK to try, OK to feel fear and OK to try several times. This persistence in itself can be a significant challenge for some children, but we know that perseverance is a strength worth developing, and that in turn builds resilience.

Reflective question 6.2

Have you seen or experienced any examples of where challenges have a positive impact on health and well-being?

Throughout all we have discussed here so far, there are two significant themes emerging that we are looking to develop in children by exposing them to risky play. First is challenge and second is competence. We want to give children the agency to develop their own competence. In the same way that we encourage children to take increasing responsibility for their own learning as they progress through their education, the same is true of their physical competencies and development. Some providers of resources and procurement channels expect children's level of competency to be proven before they are allowed access to more complex learning materials, particularly where there is a cost factor involved. However, as educators we actually have a duty and responsibility to provide children with opportunities to develop their competency. We come up against actual barriers as well as those of the perception of risk by managers, local authorities and sometimes parents.

Key takeaways

- Play – especially play with risk – is something that forms a significant part of our memories of childhood
- Injuries resulting from risky activities are rarely of significant consequence
- Mental health issues from *not* having opportunities to engage in risky, adventurous activities have greater prevalence than physical injuries from participation in such activities
- Children need challenges to develop competence and confidence

7

Things to consider for the physical environment

The outdoors must be given the same value as indoors. We're talking unbridled risk taking, collaborative, expansive play, freely chosen explorations, ultimately a deep-rooted and primal connection to the soil, trees, the earth, the sky, to our very selves.

Bottrill, 2018

This chapter

- The eight categories of risky play
- The benefits that unexpected challenges can bring
- Ensuring inclusion in play spaces
- Positive features of a risk-enhanced play space
- Proprioception – what it is and its reference to development in Early Years

The right to *all* types of play

If play is one of the most important aspects of childhood – so important that it is a right, enshrined in law in Scotland, in Article 31 of the UNCRC – then it is incumbent on us, the adults responsible for child development opportunities, to provide the richest possible environment for all aspects of play. Let's briefly revisit the Play Scotland image of all of the play types (Figure 1.2, see p. 7). We have a responsibility to ensure that our environment supports and facilitates the experience of each of these play types.

Consider in addition then, or more accurately, alongside, the eight different categories of risky play, as identified by Ellen Beate Hansen Sandseter (2007) (see Chapter 1, p. 12) – play with great heights, play with high speed, play with dangerous tools, play near dangerous elements, rough-and-tumble play and play where the children can 'disappear'/get lost and, later, by Rasmus Kleppe et al. (2017) play with impact and vicarious play.

Developing through the unexpected

While there are undoubtedly crossovers and threads linking the play types with the categories of risky play, it is also clear that our play environments need to be expansive and substantive in order to meet this need.

Niki Buchan states that: 'Supporting young children's physical play types should be of utmost importance and children show the greatest potential for wellbeing and development in natural outdoor play spaces' (2018, p. 50). She also muses that, 'when children are asked, they express a strong preference for playing outdoors' (2018, p. 47), and as the *children's voice* is so central to all we do this is an important consideration.

Contrary to a standard indoor environment, the outdoor environment naturally offers both risk and challenge. We can compare simple developmental skills such as walking, balancing, climbing or jumping. When walking in an indoor space, it is possible there may be trip or slip hazards – water on the floor, a dropped toy (do you really know pain if you've never stepped on a Lego brick barefoot?) – but by and large we know what to expect – the surface is even, with a consistent texture and mostly level. Any changes to that are learned and easily adapted for. When we go outdoors, however, we might experience a range of different surfaces underfoot. Changes in level can occur without warning, testing our balance and reactions. Trip hazards more regularly occur and are difficult to foresee. That bench or balance beam we walk on indoors and take pride in making it all the way along is a very different animal from the wobbly bridge, uneven planks, rounded log or possibly a slack line. When we enjoy the indoor climbing frame, the rungs or sections are relatively evenly spaced and therefore become predictable, the places to hold on for support are clear and easy for small hands to grip. The height is limited, together with the options of different objects of height to climb onto and jump off from. In a woodland or other varied outdoor environment with trees to climb, the skill of climbing is a greater challenge in every way, and there is no clear 'top' to where we should climb to. In each of these examples the child exploring the outdoor environment has to actively engage with the environment and consider their next steps, literally and figuratively. The environment requires a reaction, a response to the new experience. It tests the ability to maintain or regain balance; to assess, 'what next?'; to risk assess and to persevere. It can change with the seasons and sometimes daily with changes in the weather making surfaces more slippery and different to the touch. The more children are able to have this opportunity to respond to the changes and challenges of their environment, the greater they grow in confidence. Their physical and mental well-being is actively developing.

From this, then, we can see that we are actively doing a disservice to children and their development if we fail to provide an environment rich in challenge potential. By actively including aspects that engage the children in risk-assessing, we are supporting them to develop their skills at their own pace.

Reflective questions 7.1

Considering all of the different play types and risky play types, do you see those evident in your setting?

Are there opportunities to develop the environment to further facilitate all play and risky play types?

Inclusion

Inclusion should be at the centre of our environmental consideration – can all children not only access this space and all of the opportunities within it, but also find a level of challenge appropriate to them? That means providing the environment that offers a range of challenge up to your most competent children.

That statement deserves some thought – we are providing for a level of challenge for our *most* competent children. Does that not mean that we are pitching at too challenging a level for other children? We need to ensure this is not the case, and often that will happen naturally (differentiation by outcome, if you like) because the children who perhaps don't have the competency are either less likely to attempt what is too advanced for them to feel comfortable with, or they simply can't reach things that are higher, and if they can't reach then they can't climb up to it etc. This happens most organically with tree climbing – only once a child is tall enough to get themselves up onto that first branch can they then continue climbing higher. That's a progression there that's natural and, together with appropriateness of adult supervision, we can ensure different levels of challenge so that there's something for everybody.

Different competencies are challenged by the different types of balance beam experience given as an example earlier. For a child with additional needs or a very small child who has not been walking for long, just walking along a relatively narrow and stable 'bridge' might involve a significant balance factor, leading to a real sense of achievement for making it across. However, another child might run along that bridge without a second thought and would seek their challenge on the wobbly rope bridge, the fallen log or the slack line.

The point is not providing different levels of challenge for every type of activity, but rather different levels of activity for every type of challenge – the ability for every child to challenge themselves, to progress in different ways and at their own pace. We are looking for the antithesis of 'soft play'-type experiences, where children don't need to risk assess as all the protection has already been provided!

Risky features

We can dive deeper into this idea of what types of risky features we might include in our outdoor environments and the associated benefits. Examples in a children's play environment include:

1. *climbing structures*:
   - treehouses: structures built into trees with various heights and climbing options
   - rope ladders and nets: climbing nets and ladders that require balance and coordination;
2. *natural elements*:
   - rocks and logs: large rocks and logs for climbing, balancing and jumping off
   - mud pits and water areas: areas where children can play with mud and water, fostering sensory play and creativity;
3. *loose parts play*:
   - movable objects: items such as tires, planks and crates that children can move and manipulate to create their own play structures
   - natural materials: sticks, stones and leaves that children can use to build and explore;
4. *elevated platforms and bridges*:
   - high platforms: elevated play areas connected by bridges or balance beams
   - suspension bridges: bridges that sway and move, adding an element of risk;
5. *swinging and spinning equipment*:
   - rope swings: swings made from ropes hanging from trees or structures
   - spinning wheels: equipment that spins, requiring children to balance and hold on;
6. *slopes and inclines*:
   - hills and mounds: natural or artificial slopes for running up and down or rolling
   - slides on inclines: long slides that follow the natural contours of the land;
7. *exploratory paths*:
   - hidden trails: paths through bushes or wooded areas that children can explore
   - maze-like structures: structures with multiple pathways and hiding spots.

Figure 7.1 Child on a trapeze swing while another waits their turn

Proprioception

Linked to the idea of sensory development is the importance of facilitating opportunities for *proprioceptive* development in our environments. Proprioception is defined as the sense of the relative position of one's own body parts and the strength of effort being employed in movement. It is sometimes called the *sixth sense* and involves the ability to sense the position, location, orientation and movement of the body and its parts. Children naturally develop proprioception through play in a variety of ways that we don't necessarily actively plan for or lead them to. This is just how children play. For example:

1. *development of body awareness*:
   - understanding position and movement: children learn how their bodies move and how to control their movements through activities that challenge their proprioceptive sense. This includes understanding how much force to apply when jumping, climbing, or balancing
   - spatial orientation: proprioceptive input helps children understand where their bodies are in space, which is crucial for navigating their environment safely and efficiently;

2. *enhancement of motor skills*:
   - coordination and balance: activities that require balance, such as walking on a balance beam or climbing, enhance proprioceptive feedback, helping children develop better coordination and balance
   - refined motor control: engaging in various types of play helps children fine-tune their motor skills. For instance, swinging on a rope or hanging from monkey bars requires children to adjust their grip and body position, refining their motor control;
3. *risk management and confidence*:
   - assessing risk: proprioceptive input helps children gauge their abilities and assess risks more accurately. By understanding their physical limits, they can make better decisions about what they can safely attempt
   - building confidence: successfully navigating physical challenges boosts children's confidence in their physical abilities and encourages them to take on new challenges.

Proprioceptive-rich play environments might therefore include:

1. *contrasting surfaces*:
   - hard, pressure-resistant surfaces, level vs uneven ground
   - forgiving surfaces that enable digging, pushing in, burying, imprinting into, such as sand and mud
   - soft surfaces that can be enjoyed barefoot or are enjoyable to the touch, such as grass
   - crunchy leaves, needles and branches of a woodland floor that give different sensory feedback and may include trip hazards or necessitate route planning or navigation, even on the most basic level;
2. *climbing structures*:
   - rope climbing: climbing ropes or rope ladders require children to use their muscles and joints to pull themselves up, providing strong proprioceptive input
   - rock walls: climbing walls with varying difficulty levels allow children to navigate different grips and footholds, enhancing their body awareness;
3. *balancing activities*:
   - balance beams: walking on narrow beams or logs requires precise proprioceptive feedback to maintain balance
   - tightropes and slacklines: these activities challenge children to balance on a moving line, further enhancing their proprioceptive skills;
4. *swinging and spinning*:
   - swings and rope swings: swinging provides continuous proprioceptive feedback as children pump their legs and adjust their grip

- spinning equipment: equipment like roundabouts or spinning seats help children understand rotational movement and balance;

5. *jumping and landing*:
   - trampolines: jumping on trampolines requires children to control their force and balance as they bounce
   - jumping platforms: platforms of various heights for jumping off and landing on teach children to gauge distance and control their landings;
6. *heavy work activities*:
   - pushing and pulling: activities that involve pushing wheelbarrows, pulling carts, or moving large objects provide deep proprioceptive input, helping children understand their strength and movement
   - carrying objects: carrying weighted objects or backpacks during play also enhances proprioceptive awareness.

By incorporating elements that challenge and enhance proprioception, play environments can support children's physical, cognitive and emotional development, fostering a well-rounded and healthy growth process.

> Children's need for play has been globally recognised as a basic childhood right. Numerous developmental and health advantages have also been linked to children's need for outdoor risky play as a means to learn through experience. Societal trends limiting children's access to outdoor risky play opportunities combined with a culturally dominant excessive focus on safety can pose a threat to healthy child development.
>
> Brussoni et al., 2012

> Providing children with opportunities for risky play in outdoor environments increases their physical activity levels and contributes to their overall health and well-being. It is important to strike a balance between safety and allowing children to experience and learn from risk.
>
> Bundy et al., 2009

Reflective question 7.2

Thinking about the learners in your setting, how far does the environment both meet all of their needs for development through risky play features and proprioception potential and offer challenge for all?

Case study: using the environment to promote risky play

Mrs Gillian Hewitt, Depute Head Teacher

Well-being is top of our education agenda in Scotland, and we value and recognise the benefits that come from giving children the opportunity to play and experience the joy of being outside and develop resilience by taking risks in their play. Each of our classes from Nursery to Primary 7 have a dedicated hour in their weekly timetable to visit our *Woodies* for unstructured, unplanned play.

The Woodies is actually a small area of our playground which has grass and a cluster of trees and evolves with the seasons. After a storm took down a few trees we asked for them to be left untouched in order to create a wild space for the children to explore, take risks and to play freely. Teachers will often take out other provocations – tyres, ropes, tarpaulins – to enhance their play. The adults stand back and facilitate as the children are encouraged to take risks, to explore to test their boundaries.

When woodies play was introduced, we worked closely with partner providers who taught the older children about tying knots and even how to whittle wood to make woodie characters to enhance their play. This taught them how to use knives in a safe and controlled manner. When children are given space to test their own limits, they build resilience and perseverance. Failure and iteration are crucial to learning – they allow children to practise creative thinking and problem-solving.

Teachers have been on a learning journey of their own, learning when to interact rather than interfering; by taking that step back, the children are finding solutions to their problems through the key skills of teamwork, communication, problem-solving and creativity. We are seeing the impact transferring back into the classroom where the children are more motivated, focused and engaged in their more formal literacy and numeracy activities and show more resilience and positive attitudes towards their work.

Key takeaways

- As well as the 16 play types, there are eight categories of risky play; it is important that we allow for the possibility to experience them all

(Continued)

- Being faced with unexpected challenges is important
- Inclusion in play spaces requires planning
- Features of a risk-enhanced play space
- Proprioception and how it can be developed through play

8

Loose parts

I made it go so high; it was higher than me! I rolled the tyres so I could move them then Sasha helped me. She helped me push them on top. She went inside, then I went inside.

Aleksandra

This chapter

- The benefits of loose parts and the type of loose parts to include in your setting to encourage challenge
- Loose parts are versatile and encourage risk and challenge in play
- Providing a varied and plentiful supply of loose parts readily accessible reduces conflicts and supports healthy development
- Different textures, shapes and sizes of loose parts promote sensory-rich play experiences
- Loose parts enable child-led play, allowing children to take ownership of their play experiences and make independent decisions
- Loose parts foster cognitive development by encouraging children to evaluate risks, solve problems and adapt to changing situations

Introduction to loose parts

Figure 8.1 Loose parts are ideal for risky play

Loose parts don't come with instructions, and this is what makes them ideal for risk and challenge in play. They are open-ended and versatile. Children can manipulate, combine and use them in multiple ways. Loose parts invite curious investigation. Loose parts outdoors can include everyday items like plastic crates, large blocks, ropes and stones. Items like this can certainly lead to play where we are more alert. When children play with loose parts outdoors, we will often see more physical activity such as climbing, jumping, crawling and balancing.

An important lesson that I learned as a new teacher was that loose parts play needs to be readily accessible to children and also varied and plentiful – this cuts down on conflict and arguments, as well as supporting healthy development. Many outdoor loose parts, such as tyres, don't need to be put away at the end of a session, but children can quickly learn the procedures for putting away other loose parts. This helps encourage children to take care of them and involves children in decision-making.

How we position loose parts can prompt more creative play. At my outdoor playgroup, two three-year-olds ran back and forth through saris that were pinned to a low washing line for 35 minutes. They were more engaged by this resource than the other pieces of fabric that were laid on the ground. Loose parts can be a great way to encourage sensory play – children need different textures, shapes and sizes and loose parts that enable different types of movement.

As well as collecting loose parts and asking for donations, you can involve children in growing and harvesting their own loose parts. For example, bamboo grows quickly and can enable children to 'disappear'. Take care when harvesting natural loose parts from the wild. For example, you can be prosecuted in many areas of the UK for taking stones or pebbles from beaches. One holidaymaker was forced to drive hundreds of miles to return pebbles to a Cornish beach!

However, loose parts don't have to be limited to physical objects. The term 'loose parts' was coined by architect Simon Nicholson in the 1970s; in his definition, he included: smells, electricity, magnetism, gravity, gases, fluids, sounds, music, motion, chemical interactions, fire, words, concepts and ideas.

Reflective question 8.1

Reflecting on the concept of loose parts beyond physical objects, how can you incorporate non-traditional loose parts such as sounds, concepts, or ideas into your outdoor play experiences to enhance children's engagement and learning?

Loose parts and risk in play

I stepped on one bit of the wood and Charlie did go on the other end and it was all wobbly!

Jack

Loose parts were always a staple of adventure playgrounds where children were encouraged to play in ways that involved risk. The very first adventure playground, Emdrup, enabled Danish children living under Nazi occupation to create on a large scale, with free access to wood, rope, canvas, tyres, wire, bricks, pipes, rocks, logs, balls, wheels and other loose parts. Children, not adults, decided what to build or demolish, how to share tools and building materials, and how to resolve disagreements and fights.

Loose parts encourage open-ended, child-led play rather than adult-directed play. Because there are no fixed rules, loose parts are highly inclusive – each child can engage with them and use them to create challenges. Providing loose parts outdoors supports risk in play and creates an outdoor environment ripe for imagining, combining, building and experimenting. Each child's creativity is harnessed. When we see a child stacking crates to make a tall tower or enclosing a stack of tyres with ropes, we see schema play in action: children are playing in a way that suits their individual needs.

Reflective questions 8.2

Reflecting on the history of adventure playgrounds and their emphasis on children's autonomy, how might you empower children in your outdoor play space to take ownership of their play experiences with loose parts?

How might you facilitate collaborative play experiences that foster social interaction, communication and critical thinking?

Critical thinking

I got the one block under the wood plank, but when I stamped on it, it didn't move! It was too close to the middle. So, I pushed it … moved it away from the middle bit then when I jumped on it, the ball went FLYING!

George, 9

Research indicates that the flexible and adaptable nature of loose parts better stimulates cognitive development than toys with a set purpose. When children engage with loose parts, they are often engaging with uncertainty and challenge which are integral to risk in play. I run an outdoor holiday club, and this gives children the chance to explore an unfamiliar outdoor environment and a different range of outdoor loose parts. Most children get stuck in physically straight away while also engaging their brains – evaluating this new space, assessing the risks.

Through loose parts play, children investigate cause and effect relationships – how far can a ball travel when flipped by a handmade catapult? These kinds of challenges will be vastly different for each child. Working with a group of children with profound physical disabilities recently, I watched one child who cannot move her limbs independently smile each time a piece of golden fabric moved in the wind and caught the sunshine.

Having a good range of different loose parts, from fabric to cable reels to netting, can support children to develop their decision-making and judgement skills. They assess the situation and weigh up the risks and benefits. Observing play with loose parts I see children building an understanding of the potential consequences of each action, but also learning more about their own physical and emotional capabilities and finding out about the environment they are in. Through balancing on loose parts constructions and swinging on a hammock made from scrap material, children are developing risk-management skills. Often, they are making on-the-spot decisions such as where to put their foot next.

I have found that children can sometimes feel like trespassers in a play space, quickly attempting to play in their own way before it is stopped. When they are supported to manipulate parts of their environment, children start to trust their own instincts and feel they belong. Engaging in risky play with loose parts helps build children's confidence as they tackle challenges and master new skills. This can lead to a satisfying sense of accomplishment and greater self-esteem.

Key to critical thinking is adaptability – being able to adapt to changing situations and unexpected challenges. Loose parts such as wooden planks and crates can encourage children to come up with strategies, evaluate them and adjust them. For their mental health, physical and cognitive development, children need to be able to modify their play environment and loose parts are the perfect way for them to do this. For a four-year-old, a castle with towers made from cable reels and planks completely changes the playground. Children then experience a greater sense of control and responsibility.

One the most common activities that children carry out with loose parts is to build an obstacle course with varying levels of risk and challenge. They are creating their own 'problems' and solving them, and the more variables they have the better. This also builds collaborative play, promoting social interaction and communication. Children share ideas and negotiate. They work together to problem solve and reflect on their experiences. Open-ended objects stimulate a more fluid type of thinking: possibility thinking. This fluid thinking is increasingly necessary because we have to work towards pioneering solutions to issues such as climate change. We need a future society that thinks critically.

Figure 8.2 Through history, children have been drawn to loose parts play

Types of loose parts to provide

> *The Forest School area was full of dandelions. It looked amazing when we crossed the road and saw this carpet of yellow! It was totally different to last week. T and me decided to play potions when we saw all that.*
>
> Joel, 9

It's important to provide a wide range of different loose parts and a good diversity. You could consider a range of natural and man-made materials. Some ideas include:

- *logs and stumps*: these can be used to encourage climbing, balancing and jumping. Tree surgeons are often keen to get rid of pruned tree limbs and these can become building materials for children. They can also provide uneven surfaces that improve balance and coordination. As cited earlier, sensory dysfunction in children is on the rise and one of the causes could be a lack of outdoor play. This can lead to hypersensitivity, hyperactivity, clumsiness and a lack of awareness of personal space or boundaries. I have certainly seen a rise in the number of children who are presenting with sensory issues and the antidote in some cases is enabling children to encounter natural challenges such as clambering over logs. Natural obstacles can support the development of proprioception and the vestibular sense;
- *fabrics*: old sheets, blankets, or fabric pieces can be used for building shelters, hammocks and sections of obstacle courses. I was recently donated a bag of saris, and the children love to use these to create zones where they can hide and disappear;
- *sand and dirt*: these areas are essential because they offer opportunities for digging building, moulding and transformation. This is a simple way to enable children to create their own landscape. If possible, incorporate a large sand pit that children can get into. You can create this with wooden sleepers or even just a tarpaulin with temporary barriers around the edge. Children are often encouraged to keep clean and the prospect of being able to become fully absorbed in play while getting dirty and messy is thrilling for most children. Children are almost always excited by a mud pit or mud slide! Mud play is a sensory, engaging experience with an element of uncertainty. When there is a large muddy puddle, most children cannot wait to get up to a height using loose parts and launch themselves! Mud play has been shown to boost the immune system – mud contains microscopic bacteria called *mycobacterium vaccae*, increasing levels of serotonin, which calms and relaxes (Lowry et al., 2007). Getting down and dirty in the mud makes children happier. We need to get away from the idea that dirt is unhealthy, and allow children to get feet, hands and even faces in the mud!
- *a mud kitchen* encourages messy, sensory play and enables children to experiment and investigate;

- *tyres and tubing*: old tyres can provide climbing structures, tunnels, or platforms, adding a dynamic element to the play environment. They can be used for rolling, hiding, climbing through or as part of a loose parts structure. In my experience, children love to stack tyres and get inside them. (Evidently, we need to risk assess this.) Providing a range of sizes can enhance children's experience – a tractor tyre and a plank offers a climbing opportunity whereas go kart tyres present rolling opportunities;
- *tubes, pipes and guttering* can enable children to manipulate and move different materials, sometimes using height;
- *cable reels and wheels*: children love to stack and climb cable reels, as well as rolling them down slopes. Cable reels and wheels introduce an element of uncertainty and a possibility for different types of movement. When combined with wooden planks, cable reels can provide opportunities to create bridges and balancing opportunities. Planks become ramps or balance beams, encouraging movement with an element of danger. It's always interesting to see how different children approach a balancing bridge they have created using loose parts. Recently, I watched two children who had laid planks over tractor tyres. One child chose to cautiously walk over the bridge with his arms outstretched. The second child followed closely, but chose to crawl across on his hands and knees;
- *natural elements* such as water, pine cones and stones can enable creative play with risk;
- *pallets*: wooden pallets are often a staple in Early Years settings. They are so versatile and can be used for building platforms, ramps, or structures. People are often keen to get rid of pallets which makes them cost effective and sustainable. (It's important to examine pallets first for protruding nails and splintered wood.) It was amazing to watch children work with the Woodland Tribe at the Tate Modern to make amazing creations from recycled wood. Using tools, they made tunnels, ships, hiding places and magical structures;
- *cardboard boxes*: different-sized cardboard boxes can be transformed into dens, tunnels, or structures. They provide excellent opportunities for problem-solving. If you can bear it, these structures change radically in the rain!
- *ropes and nets*: most of us have certain aspects of risk in play that make us more anxious and, for me, it is ropes. However, ropes and nets open up a world of possibilities and are always used creatively by children. Ropes can be cut into shorter lengths to reduce the level of risk.

Reflective question 8.3

Reflecting on the benefits of sensory-rich play with natural elements like mud, sand and water, how might you incorporate these elements into your outdoor play space?

Case study: Watch out! Be careful!

Heleen Vis, Primary teacher in the Netherlands who has completed a master's degree with a thesis on outdoor learning

We as teachers have the tendency to protect children from any risks, but through the years I have learned to step back and let children discover their own limits. As an international school teacher at a school surrounded by forest I take my Lower Primary class (four to seven years old) out in the woods at least twice a week.

I am lucky to have access to a place in the middle of the forest that I can call our 'outdoor classroom'. Showing trust in each other is something I have seen growing in my class. In the autumn we came upon a fallen tree. It was a rainy day, muddy and the tree trunks were slippery. It would have been easy to continue our walk, not taking any risks, but the trunks were too attractive to not play on them. The children figured out for themselves which parts to avoid as they were too slippery to walk on and soon a self-devised game was created. A game in which older children were assisting the younger ones when they had to step from one log onto the other. A helping hand was offered, and they were encouraged by the older children to try to take the big step too.

Since I have put my trust in the children's play, they have had the opportunity to create fun games in which every child is involved, discovers their own limits and pushes their boundaries.

Key takeaways

- The flexible nature of loose parts enhances creativity and challenge
- Outdoor play with loose parts promotes physical development through activities such as climbing, balancing and jumping
- Having a wide range of loose parts encourages continuous engagement
- Loose parts with different textures, shapes and sizes offer rich sensory play experiences
- Loose parts play can promote autonomy, prompting decision-making
- Loose parts play often involves collaboration, enhancing social skills, communication and teamwork

9

Small spaces and expeditions

Young children are unique, active and creative learners who need the very best positive learning environments and opportunities.

Kathryn Solly, 2014

This chapter

- Discussion of the challenge of creating engaging play environments in limited outdoor spaces
- Affordances: James J. Gibson's idea that different people perceive and use their environment in unique ways
- The importance of designing playscapes that offer multiple affordances for varied types of play
- The importance of using natural elements, even in small spaces, to enhance sensory and physical play
- Productive uncertainty: the idea of incorporating uncertainty in play to stimulate curiosity and creativity

Self-determination theory

Large, natural, wild spaces are special. They encourage risk in play. Unfortunately, the research shows that children are spending less and less time outdoors and Richard Louv, author of *Last Child in the Woods*, warns that children are experiencing 'nature deficit disorder' (Louv, 2010). Without time in the 'wild', children find it more difficult to evaluate risk and make informed decisions. They can become fearful because they are moving too far out of their comfort zone. When children have regular time in wild spaces and choose how to play outdoors, they are more likely to experience trust and build competence in their abilities, fulfilling the three areas of self-determination theory: autonomy, competence and relatedness (Ryan and Deci, 2000).

Figure 9.1 Children need to develop a sense of competence

Leslie Kochanowski and Victoria Carr, based at the University of Cincinnati, stress the importance of self-determination as a human goal: 'Children deserve the right to learn in this way. It is the responsibility of adults to uphold this right by providing time for play in secure, yet unstructured environments' (Kochanowski and Carr, 2014). Kochanowski and Carr found through their research that natural environments are best in terms of self-determination theory, but this does include intentionally designed play-scapes. One of the main findings of Kochanowski and Carr's study was that loose parts and open-ended play structures are crucial for enabling healthy play. Wild, natural environments offer a wide range of loose parts so that children can follow their schemas. However, thoughtful consideration of loose parts in a small environment can replicate the effect of a wild environment.

Reflective question 9.1

Considering the research highlighting the importance of self-determination theory in outdoor play, how might you design outdoor play spaces, whether wild or intentionally designed, to foster autonomy, competence and relatedness among children?

Affordances

Sometimes I have had the opportunity to work with children in woodlands, but, more often than not, I am outdoors in a small space. We don't all have easy access to a large natural space, so how do we make sure that our intentionally designed playscape is encouraging for child-directed play that incorporates risk?

The experimental psychologist, James J. Gibson, introduced the concept of *affordances* in the 1960s, referring to the way that each person perceives the environment in a different way.

> *The value or meaning of a thing consists of what it affords.*
>
> Gibson, 1977

Affordances in the environment make an offer to a person or reveal a possible function and they are unique and different for everyone (Watkins, 2021). In considering an outdoor environment that enables children to play in a wide range of ways, we need to ensure that the space offers multiple affordances. As a side note, James' wife, Eleanor J. Gibson, was also an accomplished psychologist and is best known for her *visual cliff* experiment.

Babies were placed on a raised plexiglass structure and encouraged to crawl from a section with material covering the clear glass across a section of clear glass to a caregiver. Younger babies crawled across the apparent drop to their caregiver, but most ten-month-old babies were reluctant. The conclusion was that the older babies had better-developed depth perception and a fear of heights. However, we know that even the very young babies were fearful, with increased heart rate, but they had not grasped the consequence of falling. They only gain this understanding when they begin to crawl and experience gentle falls. Older babies look at the 'drop' and understand that they will not be able to make this descent. They are already making decisions about risk! (Adolph et al., 2014)

Figure 9.2 A healthy outdoor space offers multiple affordances

Using the natural environment

I splash! In the water! I splash!

Billy, 3

Even in a small space, the environment itself can provide some of the best loose parts in the form of weather. It frustrates me when I see areas of playground coned off because large puddles have formed. What a missed opportunity for sensory play! Water play does need to be supervised – the statistics show that drowning incidents involving very young children are mainly in the bath or in the garden pond. Water play is popular with most young children, and investing in a set of good-quality rain suits and wellies can eliminate wet and muddy clothes and enable stamping in puddles. (The adults outside also need good clothing, and this can mean the difference between a happy adult play partner and a miserable adult who can't wait to get back inside!) Vigilance is needed around water, but children learn so much from wading through water and experimenting with depth. Where there is water, there is often mud! A mud slide can offer exhilarating sliding opportunities.

One nursery I work with has a beautiful lake a short walk away; walking to streams and ponds obviously requires close supervision and carefully thought-out risk assessment, but also gives children enriching experiences. Children learn to navigate different terrains and quickly learn the boundaries. The journey to a different location can provide as much enjoyment as play at the destination, and when young children can move at their preferred pace, they can be playful with natural materials and enjoy different sensory experiences along the way (Watkins, 2021).

Play outside in all weathers builds children's evaluation and decision-making skills. I remember watching a child walking across the wooden beam of a play structure in winter, pushing a foot forwards onto the frosty surface to test the slipperiness, while holding tight to the rope above. Ice play has elements of danger, and most children are driven to smash up larger sections of ice into smaller chunks! Children (and many adults!) are compelled to handle ice, manipulate it, transport it and melt it. We are going to experience more extreme weather conditions in the future and outdoor play in different conditions can help children cope with this. Rewilding Britain defines rewilding as: 'The large-scale restoration of ecosystems to the point where nature is allowed to take care of itself' (Rewilding Britain, n.d.). Through rewilding our outdoor spaces, and rewilding the children in our care, we are reconnecting them with natural elements and enabling them to engage with uncertainty.

Close to where I live, a huge oak tree, over 100 years old, came down in the middle of a housing estate following a storm. What was fascinating to see was that as soon as this magnificent tree was felled, children of all ages were drawn to play on and around its multiple branches. It has now become a permanent play feature and the playground next to it is often empty – the children choose to play on a structure with more potential for uncertainty. Not many of us have room for a huge felled oak tree, but close to this tree is a selection of upright logs from the tree, attached together with a piece of strong wire. This small, uneven natural resource is popular and elicits a wide range of different types of play. Long logs laid on the ground and short log sections standing up can support risk in play. This can be a good starting point for tree climbing. However small the outside space, the natural environment can be represented. Here are some ideas:

- shrubs and herbs (rosemary grows prolifically)
- small trees
- a sand pit (preferably that children can get into)
- access to water
- mud kitchen/mud area
- large sticks and branches
- different levels created using small sections of railway sleepers
- 'gullies' with stones to define the edges
- straw bales.

Rewilding the space can enable children to hide away, an important part of risk in play. Young children don't need big spaces to experience that feeling of being away from adult surveillance. Loose parts such as material and sticks can enable children to construct their own hiding places.

Reflective question 9.2

How can you incorporate elements of uncertainty and productive uncertainty into the outdoor environment to stimulate children's curiosity, creativity and exploration, even in small or urban spaces?

Natural elements

> *We are lucky to have all these trees in our playground. They were planted by other children 40 years ago. We can shelter under them when it's hot and sometimes we are allowed to climb them.*
>
> Owen, 9

Fire is one of the natural elements identified in Sandseter's categories of risky play. If space allows, we can enable children to learn about lighting, building and maintaining fires and support them to safely interact with fire. At one setting, I have an arrangement with the local parish council to use a piece of common land over the road where a fire circle has been created. It can be more straightforward to travel to another setting to experience fire. Many settings now enable children in Early Years to make their own toast when they are hungry, and this can be a first step to engaging with heat safely.

We can also consider ways to offer different surfaces and gradients. In one school where I taught Reception, there was a synthetic grass-covered slope which was endlessly popular. It was fascinating to see the children climb the slope and roll down themselves or launch wheeled vehicles or loose parts. In the same outdoor area there was a small, steep slope next to the fence and this was a honeypot area for children. Even the smallest created 'hill-ock' will give young children the much-needed chance to test themselves. Children need that opportunity to climb, roll and slide.

Climbing

I climbed up with Louie. We climbed up it. And we jumped off!

Sammie

In a small space, a climbing wall can boost climbing skills. A-frames and child-sized ladders are fantastic for independent climbing. Loose parts such as tyres and planks enable children to create bridges and ramps and explore different heights. Loose parts can also enable children to balance, roll and slide. Children instinctively want to climb, seeking the highest point they can access (Watkins, 2021); Froebel described climbing a tree as 'discovering a new world' (Froebel, 1887). Expeditions to nearby areas may enable children to climb trees, building important focus and concentration skills as well as physical skills. It's worth starting off on low heights and avoiding lifting children into trees. The more practice the better – every climbing opportunity helps children learn more about body awareness and balance. Each time they climb, children are thinking about where to place their feet until it becomes more instinctive. It is natural for children to feel a little scared and this fear can help them make better decisions.

Children often want to progress from climbing to jumping and it can be unnerving to see children launch themselves into space! However, assessing heights and learning to land safely are important skills. You could consider using mats outdoors, but take care not to instil a false sense of security because children need to make appropriate judgements.

Reflective questions 9.3

How can you design and incorporate features in your outdoor space to encourage children's physical development, exploration and experimentation with movement?

Specifically, how could you incorporate climbing opportunities into your outdoor play space?

Swinging

Children need to experience swinging and hanging, speed and heights, for healthy development. Incorporating removable swings and hammocks attached to a wooden structure can be a good way to enable this in small spaces. A rope swing can be a more natural alternative to a playground swing and will provide plenty of opportunities for risky play. The rope swing area in one setting where I worked was always popular and it built social skills because children needed to communicate, take turns and listen carefully.

Figure 9.3 Swinging is immensely beneficial and engaging

Tools

Even in the smallest space, tools can be introduced. You may not have room for a permanent full-size workbench, but you can have sessions where tools are available. For example, palm drills and boards can be provided so that children can learn how to drill holes in wood slices. A folding sawhorse can enable children to saw wood slices. Teaching children to whittle wood using vegetable peelers can be done in a small space. Here are some tips for whittling:

- use green wood because wood that has lain on the ground for some time is much harder to whittle; be aware that the peeler can get stuck or even jump off knots in sticks;
- the child should wear a glove on their non-dominant hand;
- the child needs to be sitting down or kneeling to whittle;
- model picking the peeler up by its handle;
- ensure that each child has an arm's length 'bubble' when peeling;
- ensure that children peel away from themselves, paying close attention at all times and pointing the stick downwards;
- make sure peelers are kept out of reach when not in use.

Reflective question 9.4

How can you integrate opportunities for children to engage in hands-on, experiential learning with tools and materials to foster their curiosity, problem-solving abilities and confidence in exploring new skills and techniques?

Key takeaways

- Effective playscape design can turn even small areas into rich, engaging environments
- It's vital to ensure that the outdoor space offers a range of affordances to cater to children's diverse needs and interests
- Integrating natural materials like water, mud and trees can significantly enhance children's development
- Allowing children to engage in controlled risk-taking fosters decision-making and problem-solving skills
- Providing hands-on learning opportunities with tools can build children's confidence and skillsets

10

The emotional environment

Life is best organized as a series of daring ventures from a secure base.

Bowlby, 1988

This chapter

- The natural 'feel-good' benefits from active play
- How an environment can promote trust and feelings of safety
- Adults' responses influence children's emotions and feelings of security
- The importance and value of weapon play and its place in our settings

Supporting children through the environment

Having considered the physical environment, the resources and other spaces, we have identified that they have a significant impact on the holistic development of the whole child – not only their physical development, but also their emotional and social development. We have to consider, then, these developmental aspects in terms of the environment we offer. Are we consciously considering the emotional environment that we are providing for our children?

The Whole-Brain Child (Bryson and Siegal, 2012) contains lots of reminders about the connection between the emotions in the brain and the body, encouraging movement as an important way to help to deal with negative emotions. It also talks about engaging the full range of senses in order to help regulation. The Decider Skills programme uses a grounding technique called Right Now, often better known as 54321, to look outside ourselves to reduce stress:

5 Things I can see/imagine right now

4 Things I can hear/imagine right now

3 Things I can touch/imagine right now

2 Things I can smell/imagine right now

1 Deep slow breath, the focus on your breath

When we engage this technique in the outdoors it appears to have a much more significant impact due to the ability to connect with the calmness of the natural world. Focusing on hearing the wind blowing, the fire crackling or the birds calling has an undoubtedly more calming impact than the sometimes-overwhelming sounds that bounce off the walls indoors. Not to mention, if we are outdoors engaging in challenging play activities, we are far more likely to be producing natural dopamine, meaning we are feeling happier and less inclined to stress responses in the first place. An active child has more feelings of joy and desire to keep moving.

The emotional responses and the emotional wellbeing of children is impacted by both the physical environment and the approach of the caregivers in that environment – how we facilitate the children's freedoms to play and have adventures. The emotional environment plays a crucial role in either supporting or creating barriers to risky play for children. Here are some examples of how the emotional environment impacts risky play, you can probably come up with more from your own experiences.

A supportive emotional environment promotes:

1. *encouragement and trust*:
   - positive reinforcement: when caregivers and educators encourage children to take risks and praise their efforts, it builds children's confidence and willingness to engage in risky play
   - trust: a trusting relationship between children and caregivers allows children to feel secure in exploring their limits, knowing they have support if needed;
2. *emotional safety*:
   - feeling valued: children who feel valued and respected are more likely to take healthy risks because they trust their environment and the people in it
   - open communication: when children feel they can communicate their fears and successes, they are more likely to push their boundaries in play;
3. *role modelling*:
   - observing adults: when adults model risk-taking behaviour and demonstrate how to assess and manage risks, children learn these skills through observation
   - shared experiences: participating in risky play with children can show them that risk-taking is a normal and manageable part of life;

4. *balanced approach to safety*:
   - reasonable risk-taking: an environment that promotes reasonable risk-taking without unnecessary restrictions helps children understand the difference between safe and unsafe risks
   - supportive supervision: adults provide supervision that supports independence while ensuring safety, allowing children to explore and take risks within a safe framework.

An environment may instil barriers to emotional development if it exhibits:

1. *overprotectiveness*:
   - fear of injury: adults who are overly concerned with safety may restrict risky play, leading children to develop a fear of taking risks
   - helicopter supervision: excessive supervision and intervention can prevent children from developing their own risk assessment and management skills;
2. *negative reinforcement*:
   - criticism and discouragement: criticising or discouraging children from taking risks can lead to a lack of confidence and fear of failure
   - focus on failure: an environment that focuses on the negative outcomes of risk-taking can make children overly cautious and reluctant to engage in risky play;
3. *lack of emotional support*:
   - absence of trust: without a supportive emotional environment, children may feel insecure and anxious about taking risks
   - isolation: children who do not feel emotionally supported may avoid risky play due to fear of judgement or lack of encouragement;
4. *inconsistent responses*:
   - mixed messages: inconsistent responses from caregivers regarding risky play can confuse children about what is acceptable and safe, leading to either overly risky behaviour or excessive caution
   - unpredictability: unpredictable reactions from adults can create an environment of uncertainty, deterring children from exploring risky play.

Reflective question 10.1

What regulation techniques are employed in your setting and how does the environment support those, and support children emotionally in general?

Features of an emotionally supportive environment

We can consider how different environments with contrasting characteristics support children's emotional development to a greater or lesser degree. In an emotionally supportive environment, you might see a well-designed play area with climbing structures, balancing beams and natural elements encouraging children to take risks in a controlled environment. Caregivers provide guidance and support, allowing children to explore their limits safely. Creating a supportive emotional environment involves providing encouragement, trust and reasonable boundaries, all of which help children develop the confidence and skills needed to engage in healthy risky play.

Conversely, in an environment that might (however unintentionally) promote barriers to emotional support, you might see overly sterile play spaces with overly safe, predictable equipment and excessive safety rules, which may inhibit children's natural inclination to take risks, leading to less engagement and exploration. Where an environment is characterised by overprotectiveness, negative reinforcement and lack of support this can inhibit children's natural risk-taking behaviours, impacting their development negatively.

One type of play that frequently stirs up discussion and will often have people with very strong views either 'for' or 'against' is weapon play. How frequently in your setting does a stick become a 'gun' … frequently accompanied by 'pow pow' noises and talk of 'killing'? It can be unnerving and uncomfortable as an adult caring for young children to see and hear that. Where do you sit on that discussion? Is weapon play allowed in your setting, or is it 'we don't play with guns here'? In the book of that title, Penny Holland (2003) explores the deep-rooted feelings that weapon play can evoke. Firstly, she asserts that the question as to *why* this debate tends to revolve around boys and *why* it is more frequently boys than girls who choose weapon play has not yet been answered. However, because that gender issue does exist, it is therefore boys who are most frequently penalised for trying to express themselves through this chosen type of play. This can in turn generate low self-esteem and negative gender identity. That doesn't sound like a very emotionally supportive environment. When I used to be firmly in the anti-gun-play camp that made me extremely uncomfortable. That was a discomfort that I sat with, as I read the book and challenged where my own feelings about this came from and why. I suspect this is a debate that will exist for some time yet! Perhaps the important outcome from the debate is not whether or not we support this type of play, but rather *how* we either facilitate or discourage it – which can have a positive or negative impact.

Reflective questions 10.2

Can you picture environments that you feel have invited children to feel free to play as they please, to explore and discover?

Are there any aspects of a play environment or way of playing which challenge you?

Key takeaways

- The type of environment we facilitate reflects our approach to risk in play
- The way we model our feelings about different types of play and the environment has an impact on children's feelings of emotional security within that environment
- The environment we create impacts children's emotional development

11

Staff development: hearing and supporting staff

The most valuable resource that all teachers have is each other. Without collaboration our growth is limited to our own perspectives.

Robert John Meehan, 2010

This chapter

- Some of the most often-expressed staff concerns
- The benefits of listening to fears of your team, encouraging sharing and discussion
- Fears are expected, accepted and supported
- Planning to avoid a missing child scenario

There's no such thing as bad weather ...

Ask any practitioner in an outdoors setting what their greatest fear or concern was before they took on their outdoor role and the most common theme will be the weather. Having also worked with a lot of staff in predominantly indoor settings delivering outdoor training I can say that is also the most common fear among staff! There is no getting away from the fact that there is a huge difference between the clothing you might choose to walk the dog in less than clement weather (or indeed that the dog can wait for their walk until the weather clears up a bit), and clothing that you would want to be wearing if you know you are going to be outdoors for four, six, eight … hours.

Many parents have the same concerns about sending their little ones to fully outdoor settings, and even on occasion to an indoor setting on a day that may be colder or wetter than they might be used to. As all settings are now developing their outdoor spaces and embracing spending more time outdoors, some parents are resisting this move and requesting that their children not be exposed to some more challenging weather conditions. Why? Because they see it as a risk. Somehow, we have reached a point where weather is seen as being 'good' or 'bad'. 'Bad' weather is to be avoided because there is the perception that it may cause harm. A brief look into any medical journal or guide will remind us that this is not the case – we don't become ill because of the cold or wet weather, but those conditions can exacerbate the circulation of viruses. We have less naturally occurring vitamin D and a combination of factors make it appear as if the weather is the cause. The real issue is usually the fluctuation in weather conditions together with our central heating and spending more time indoors with more people (crowded trains and buses instead of walking everywhere, pubs and indoor meetings instead of beer gardens and gathering outside).

Returning to the issue of the clothing we might choose when we know we are going to be outside for several hours, it is vital that settings lead the way in supporting staff (and parents) to understand what types of clothing are appropriate. You will doubtless have heard the saying, 'There's no such thing as bad weather, just inappropriate clothing.' That saying has been attributed to individuals such as Sir Ranulph Fiennes and Sir Billy Connolly, and to entire nations (as a Norwegian or Danish saying), but actually appears to have originated from hillwalker Alfred Wainwright in his 1973 book, *A Coast to Coast Walk*. While I would argue with the merits of that saying when it comes to hillwalking (the hill isn't going anywhere, but in such a remote environment the weather just might make the walk too risky so my benefit–risk assessment would suggest I delay the walk to a different day with different weather conditions), for outdoor play it is almost entirely appropriate ('almost' because exceptions include lightning storms and woodlands in high winds). As it was not the intention to devote an entire chapter to the weather, let's summarise the advice for appropriate clothing for all weathers …

- *cotton* = cool (or cold in winter, and if it gets wet it stays wet) – avoid, for the most part;
- *wicking* = warm and dry, therefore perfect for base layers next to the skin;
- *wool* = warm (but can also provide balance year-round as it is thermo-regulating);
- ***layers*** = law!!! (not literally, but far and away the best way to be prepared for any weather; bottoms as well as tops).

A great resource giving more detail on this is the Inspiring Scotland practitioner tips: 'What to wear' (Thrive Outdoors, 2020).

Hear the fear

If being adequately prepared for the weather is a fear (for children or staff), we should ensure that this and any other fear is appropriately managed and supported in settings to facilitate the best possible experiences for the children. Staff need to be entirely confident in their benefit–risk analysis and their own capacity to support play activities – or they themselves can be a risk factor.

Daisy manages out of hours (primarily breakfast club and after school childcare) settings and recently conducted some research with her staff team around some of their understanding of what risky play is and their concerns around facilitating risky play. Some of the staff's comments in the early stages of the research were interesting and can be imagined to be representative of lots of staff in Early Years and wraparound care settings. Comments included:

- 'Risky play is children experimenting with their limits during play'
- 'Risky play helps to build children's resilience and push boundaries'
- 'I think risky play is good for the children's well-being'
- 'Children can have fun while taking risks'
- 'Loose parts encourages children to develop higher levels of critical thinking which are needed for taking risks'
- 'Parents' expectations are hard to manage. I don't feel like they know enough about the benefits of risky play'
- 'I feel staff are lacking in confidence when trying to provide risky play'
- 'It is better now we do risk–benefits instead of risk assessments'
- 'It would be better to have specific risky play training rather than just play in general'
- 'We should get the children more involved in assessing the risks involved'.

It is really heartening to know that in this study and through many other conversations with Early Years staff about the idea of risky play, almost all will speak positively about the benefits to the children of being able to include elements of risk in their play. What is particularly interesting is that often there is then a dichotomy between what is said in these conversations and how that actually translates to the play pedagogy. Clearly, they had the knowledge, but what this highlights is the importance of experience and practical learning/training opportunities. Initially, Daisy had thought that differences in views and practice may be linked to health and safety awareness driving concerns, but it became clear that the staff's views were shaped far more by their own life experiences and their learned experiences in settings. Education Scotland highlights exactly these influences: 'These differences may be influenced by the existence of health and safety legislation, by deeply held views and practices in our ELC settings' (Education Scotland, 2020). A practitioner I spoke to highlighted that in his experience this difference in understanding and practice, as well as differences of views about what risky play means and its value, leads to a lack of opportunities for children. In trying to develop this area further he has introduced risk assessing with the children in the setting, but ultimately describes the decision as being taken out of his hands. Despite having some fantastic physical features in one setting, children were not allowed to use the features to play on/with due to the perceived risks. So, it is not only staff on the ground who can struggle with the fear and challenge of facilitating risk as part of children's play, but also sometimes it is the management who make decisions that prevent the development of risky play situations. Staff development is therefore also limited.

In a different setting, this same practitioner is still pursuing the development of risky play opportunities; his action plan includes in-service training, trying to increase and encourage opportunities for risky play in the existing outdoor area and looking at using a local country park to expand their possibilities. The idea of making the best use of space is one which can in itself be a source of fear or concern for staff. In Daisy's research, one staff member noted that 'some of us don't live in this area, so we need to know it better to utilise the space more'.

Reflective questions 11.1

What fears have you experienced, either as a practitioner or among your colleagues or team? How have those fears been supported and has the outcome been positive?

The ultimate fear? A missing child

This key area – knowing, being familiar with and understanding the available space – is one that Louise and her team at Little Bugs nursery have explored in depth. Their setting is on a huge expanse of land, which includes a residential centre for outdoor and adventurous activities and large areas of woodland, open grassy areas, undulating slopes and dips. Plenty to keep little ones enthralled and potentially literally lost in their play. The nursery has a *basecamp*, that is fenced and secure, but they also utilise the wider estate. Louise explained to me that one of the most significant challenges for new staff members has been embracing the concept of allowing children to explore and experience play in solitude, including the sensation of being lost and disappearing. This links back to Ellen Sandseter's sixth identified category of risky play – play where children can 'disappear' or get lost. Louise identified that for new staff members who had the safety and well-being of children as their primary concern, the idea of children exploring freely without constant supervision was a source of some anxiety. In this case, the anxiety stemmed from the fear of being held responsible for any mishaps, so the idea of children not being visible at all times was a major hurdle for staff. INSET training, with Sandseter's categories of risky play as the framework, was undertaken with the whole team. Louise observed that this process helped to reduce the anxiety among staff, who began to appreciate that risky play, including moments of solitude, is essential for fostering resilience, problem-solving skills and independence in children. Louise goes on to explain:

> Additionally, we made clear links between risky play and our curriculum, highlighting how these activities align with learning through play and schemas. We demonstrated how risky play supports various learning outcomes, such as physical development, cognitive growth and emotional resilience. By weaving these concepts together, staff could see how risky play naturally fits into our educational framework and enhances overall learning experiences.

The Care Inspectorate in Scotland launched their SIMOA campaign in 2021, in response to a number of incidents where children had wandered away from an Early Years group or setting.

The SIMOA campaign features a friendly cartoon elephant and uses the following:

> *Safety*: Be alert to all potential risks in your setting.
>
> *Inspect*: Look around and inspect the environment to make sure a child can't leave an area without staff or their parent/carer.
>
> *Monitor*: Regularly check that all children are accounted for, particularly when they are outside, on outings or using transport.
>
> *Observe*: Observe children and think about their feelings and emotional security – use these observations to support children to feel loved and secure.
>
> *Act*: Assess and take action to keep children safe.
>
> Care Inspectorate, 2021

Having had a child wander away from their group in a setting I was managing, I know first-hand how easy it is for the tiniest lapse in any aspect of this to lead to a situation which has your heart in your mouth, and nobody will have consciously done anything 'wrong'. Practitioners need to have supportive processes and structures in place to help them to safely manage their groups at all times; Louise says that effectively utilising this template played a crucial role in Little Bugs' approach:

> Rather than eliminating the element of risky play where children might feel lost, we incorporated SIMOA to support and document these experiences safely. This tool helped staff feel more secure in allowing children the freedom to explore, knowing that there were structured protocols in place.

Starting with their fenced-in basecamp, the area was deliberately designed to allow for children being out of sight of staff in any number of spaces. Play spaces around corners, screened zones, additional play structures in the middle of open spaces – these all contribute to an area that is rich in play opportunities that meet all of the risky play categories and overall play types. As staff became comfortable with this set-up, they were reassured that the environment was safe for children to engage in solitary play. This incremental approach was key to building confidence among staff members. Communication between staff is supported by the use of walkie-talkies, so they never need to shout to share information. Louise reports that their efforts have had evident positive results, saying:

> staff confidence has significantly increased, and the children have become adept at understanding and respecting boundaries. This has greatly supported their play and development. We are now able to conduct whole nursery outings to expansive areas of our site, splitting the children into smaller groups for safety. We use SIMOA during these outings as part of a check list, and the children are familiar with the SIMOA elephant, which has streamlined the process and made it enjoyable for all.

Figure 11.1 Children playing 'alone'

The experiences of these Early Years colleagues who have kindly shared their stories highlight the importance of open communication and support to facilitate risky play. There is a broad knowledge of the importance of access to this type of play, and we need to work together to ensure it is delivered in a way that everyone is comfortable with. Through the effective use of tools like SIMOA and comprehensive staff training, settings can create a supportive and nurturing environment that benefits both the children and the staff.

Reflective questions 11.2

Have you ever experienced this scenario of a missing child or even a 'near miss'?

How was the incident followed up and what was the learning from it?

What key processes are in place to reduce the likelihood of it happening?

Case study: risky play in practice

Emma Green, Wild and Green Outdoor Learning

Lighting fires, climbing trees and using knives are all activities I never have to encourage children to do. From the moment the children see my face in the morning, they ask, 'are we making a fire today?', 'can I whittle today?'. There is nothing more motivating for a child than something that seems 'dangerous'. From the toddler that crawls towards the flickering flames with a look of awe on his face, to the teenager who won't engage in anything other than whittling, they all seem to be intrinsically drawn to risky play.

During my eight years as a primary school teacher, I became fascinated by the way children seemed to thrive in the outdoor classroom. This led me to complete a master's degree in which I studied the impact of outdoor learning on children's resilience. I was able to observe risky play in alternative settings, both in the UK and in Scandinavia, and undertook a study based upon the experiences of my EYFS class. This was where I discovered how important risky play is in the development of the whole child. I have now been running my outdoor learning business for over three years, working with schools, community groups and families. This has led me to draw even stronger conclusions on the impact of risky play.

Most of us can describe joyful memories of risky play from our own childhoods. I remember building dens, tree-climbing and rough-and-tumble play. However, despite these fond memories held by many adults, children today are spending significantly less time taking part in risky and outdoor play, both in their educational institutions and at home. This is a problem. Preventing

(Continued)

children from taking part in risky play lowers the possibility of them encountering challenge and failure, therefore giving them fewer opportunities to develop resilience. Less exposure to risk as a child is also linked to a higher probability of experimenting with more inappropriate risks, like drugs and alcohol, in their teens or adulthood. There might be a simple explanation for this decline in risky play. In recent years, society in the UK has developed a *risk-averse culture.* The word 'risk' now seems to equate to 'danger' for many parents and professionals. Children have never been safer, but is their safety compromising their development?

I have found that language is the key to changing adults' perception of risk and how they supervise children when risk-taking. From the way they phrase their warnings, 'be careful!', to how they present their body language (anxious, watching too closely), adults are often quite open to adapting the way they respond to their children exploring risky play. Perhaps when a child is climbing a tree, instead of 'be careful!' you could try 'remember to test the branches' or 'do you feel safe?' This comes across to the child as more of a reminder from an adult who trusts them to make their own choices than an unhelpful nagging. Often, helping adults rephrase their language around risk can be the small step that makes a huge difference. This sort of language provides the child with helpful advice which will one day become their internal voice, helping them to be safer in the future when the adult isn't around.

Real tools create real results, and therefore command real respect. I have heard many more stories of children cutting themselves with school scissors, or breaking an arm on the concrete playground, than during an outdoor learning session involving their 'riskier' counterparts of knives and tree-climbing. Even the most challenging children seem to have the concentration for whittling, firelighting, or working out the safest route up a tree. Children concentrate harder and for longer on things they actively want to do. This concentration leads them to become safer and more engaged, which actually reduces the risk compared to a mundane task, using pretend or 'safety' tools. When real tools are introduced slowly, methodically and with clear safety boundaries, children are so motivated to use them that they are more inclined to behave sensibly. I have used whittling knives and firelighters with children whom the teachers have 'warned' me about: 'Don't let him use a knife!' And, honestly, they respected the tools as much as, or perhaps even more than, their mainstream peers due to their sheer desire to be allowed to use them.

Risk is a key theme in outdoor learning, as it is in life! Whether a child is learning to use a new tool or climb a tree, the mastery of risky and adventurous activities builds resilience, intrinsic motivation, problem-solving and communication skills. It is particularly important for adults to allow children to take appropriate risks and use positive language around risky play as this leads to the development of key skills children will take with them back into the classroom, their home lives and their futures. Additionally, this will help us create a positive mindset among the general public on risky play.

Key takeaways

- Ways to support staff and children (and parents) to be comfortable in every type of weather
- How a team might approach discussions around fears of risky or even simply outdoor play
- Planning to avoid a missing child situation

12

Getting parents on board

The nursery has been clear from the start about their ethos. The children are outside in all weathers and my daughter has made great progress there.

Parent

This chapter

- Strong partnerships with parents and carers to enable children to take healthy risks in their play
- Enabling dialogue to address concerns and convey the ethos of risk in play
- Making parents and carers feel they are part of the discussion
- Working together with parents and carers for collaborative advocacy
- Embracing the challenge of educating parents about the benefits of risky play

Introduction

Good partnership with parents and carers is crucial, but we can sometimes feel pressure to limit the environment or the activities to minimise criticism and complaints. As Head of School, all complaints would eventually come to me, and I found that communication and relationships were key. We need to have that continual dialogue where parents and carers feel they are heard, but also understand the ethos of the setting and why we make certain decisions. It's important to swiftly address any concerns or misconceptions parents may have about risk in play.

As a parent myself, I appreciated that my children's teachers listened to my concerns and that there was a two-way dialogue. As previously stated, parents and carers are the experts on their child; I find it fascinating to learn about the way my students play at home. For example, the parents of a child I taught in Reception told me that she spent every weekend climbing trees. At school, I found she was able to coach other children who had less experience.

Working with parents and carers can be an opportunity to co-campaign to address some of the dangers that face our children such as traffic, air pollution and mental health issues. That partnership can help reduce the risks facing young children in our society. Involving parents and carers in the decision-making process can help them to feel more involved and have a better understanding of the need for risk in play. Be brave and actively seek their input!

Reflective questions 12.1

How can you foster open communication and collaboration to address concerns and misconceptions about risk in play?

How can you encourage parents and carers to share their own experiences and insights about how their children have benefited from engaging in risky play?

Convey the passion!

As advocates for risky play, we have to risk telling uncomfortable truths about risky play.

Aunt Annie's Childcare, n.d.

Highlighting success stories and positive outcomes related to risk in play experiences can work well and encouraging parents to share their own stories of how their children have benefited from engaging in risk in play can support that two-way dialogue. If you are clear as a staff team about your stance on risk in play, it becomes much easier to explain your ethos to parents and carers. Do you have regular discussions on how and why children at your setting challenge themselves through play?

Figure 12.1 Communicating the benefits of risky play can be impactful

Many practitioners are firm about their ethos. 'Aunt Annie', who runs Aunt Annie's Childcare, has the following advice:

> To get the message across, we also have to take some risks. As advocates for risky play, we have to risk telling uncomfortable truths about risky play to parents who don't want to hear them. Who may see our comments as a negative judgment on their parenting style. Who may think us lazy or uncaring for wanting their children to engage in play that might hurt them. To achieve change we must be patient, be committed, and above all be brave. Are you brave enough to try to change parents' thinking about risky play? Start changing what you display in your daily photos. Here's an uncomfortable truth about risky play: children who want to take a risk will frequently do it behind your back if you forbid it in your presence. Share that fact with these parents. You have to start a conversation with even the most resistant parents. You have to make them see that controlled risk is desirable, because otherwise you either get uncontrolled risk or no risk.
>
> Aunt Annie's Childcare, n.d.

Many parents will have fond memories of play – invite them to reflect on their own memories of play with risk.

Emphasising the benefits of risk

When you climb the climbing wall, you need to use your muscles, but you have to use your mind too. So, it's good!

Annabel, 9

It's important to explain to parents and carers specific ways in which challenging play is beneficial. For example, children need to develop an awareness of how their bodies work and how to evaluate and manage risks. James Hedlund states that people adjust their behaviour to compensate for perceived safety improvements, engaging in riskier actions: this concept is known as *risk compensation*. Children may worry less about hurting themselves because of safety surfaces, leading to an increase in injuries (Hedlund, 2000).

Through social media or other sharing platforms we have an opportunity to share with parents and carers the importance of risk in play for building resilience, problem-solving skills and self-confidence. Photos of children challenging themselves in their play can have a powerful impact and convey the deep immersion and engagement. Through the photos we share, we can also be advocates for outdoor play in all weather.

Sharing research findings and expert opinions on the positive impact of risk in play on children's physical, cognitive and emotional development can be thought-provoking and spark discussions. You could consider offering workshops for parents and carers to explain what risk in play entails and the different forms it can take. Most crucial of all is maintaining open and transparent communication with parents and carers about your philosophy and approach to play in your setting.

Reflective question 12.2

How might you utilise social media and sharing platforms to share photos, research findings and expert opinions with parents and carers, fostering a deeper understanding and appreciation for the value of risk in play?

Children's rights

The game at this age is not just playing, it is the highest level of child development; it is very serious and has deep meaning. Cultivate and nourish it. Protect and look after it.

Froebel Trust, n.d

A golden thread running through this book is that risk in play is linked to trusting children and supporting them on their journey rather than taking charge and putting ourselves in the role of 'expert'. Many parents welcome this disruption of the traditional teacher/child hierarchy, but some want to hear the reasoning behind this approach. In conversations with parents and carers about risky play, I often find myself coming back to Froebel's principle of: *freedom with guidance*. It's about putting to one side our assumptions and starting where the child is, enabling the child to learn at their own pace, exploring, investigating and discovering.

Figure 12.2 Supporting children on their journey

Froebellian education focuses on the development of the whole child – physically, mentally and emotionally. The role of the educator was seen by Froebel as absolutely crucial. Key to this role is working to understand and respect the natural inclinations of children while acting as play facilitators, providing an environment where children can explore, experiment and learn through play. Followers of Froebel's philosophy support children to connect with the natural environment and understand their place in the natural environment and in the community. To thrive in any community, children need to learn skills such as cooperation and respect for others. Recently, I was observing three children in the wild area of the playground. One child was climbing a low tree, and another child began to climb up too. The third child, who was watching, said to the second child: 'It's too hard for her to get down now because you are in the way.' The second child looked around for a branch to move to in order to enable the first child to get back down, but this wasn't possible. He stepped back down to the ground and waited for the first child to come back down and then started to climb the tree himself. For Froebel, a key role of educators was to provide appropriate support and guidance to help children progress through developmental stages (scaffolding this when needed). In the situation above, I was ready to step in, but I didn't need to.

Being a play facilitator, supporting children to push themselves and make sense of their experiences requires time and sensible ratios. As a Reception teacher, I sometimes had the whole class without a TA, so the approach had to be more focused on guidance rather than freedom. This was frustrating to say the least. Part of our role is to model to parents and carers that delicate balance between nurturing a child's natural curiosity and offering guidance when needed. In the end, it's about partnership: 'Parents should not fear because they do not know how to teach their children – let them imitate the child's example … become children with the child, learners with the learner' (Froebel Trust, n.d.).

Reflective question 12.3

What are some strategies we as educators could implement to ensure that we cultivate, nourish, protect and prioritise play experiences?

Case study: how can risk in play benefit children with a disability or SEN?

Lea Archer is an Independent Therapeutic Forest Practitioner, passionate about Early Years and SEND

I enjoy running Therapeutic Forest School sessions for children who benefit from smaller groups in a non-school setting. I am working with J, a five-year-old

(Continued)

boy who is on a long waiting list for speech and language support. He has a hand deformity (symbrachydactyly) which he is becoming more aware of as he gets older and ADHD traits which run in his family.

J and I have developed a good relationship over the last two years. I've got to appreciate his interests and energetic personality. As we developed our connection, I learned about what made him frustrated, his anxieties, triggers and how to diffuse them. I observed that he stuck rigidly to playing with cars, trains and building blocks. He found it difficult to play alongside a large group of children and would rather work alone sometimes. I quickly realised that he needed opportunities to let off steam before he could transition to any other activity, so he needed to spend a time running around the garden, throwing himself on the swing and sliding down the slide into the sandpit before we could move on.

I know that he sometimes finds the school environment difficult, but I get to see how he flourishes in the woods when we are on our forest adventures. I don't pressure him because our activities are always child-led and spontaneous. J likes the physical act of hammering the tent pegs to make our shelter before we start looking for mini-beasts and mushrooms in the undergrowth and finding the perfect walking stick. He finds his own way to use and strengthen his hand when he has time and space to work it out.

We make dens made from sticks and branches which we drag behind us because they are so heavy. J is very particular about construction and has many suggestions and directions about our build. He's free to run, jump, climb, splash in puddles and squelch through mud with the only rule being that he stays in sight. He listens, asks questions and is far more talkative when outside. I believe he benefits from 'side-by-side' interactions which happen naturally when we are walking. There's no pressure to make eye contact, which can be intimidating, and there's always something interesting to see or climb under or over while chatting! J hasn't had any meltdowns on our adventures. Forest School sessions are perfect for risk in play activities and tick every developmental box.

(For support for children with a limb difference, see Reach: www.reach.org.uk/.)

Balance

Throughout the whole process of communicating with parents and carers about risk in play, there needs to be a focus on encouraging parents and carers to understand and respect their child's abilities and preferences. As well as warning against overprotection, it's also important to ensure that children are not forced to take risks in play. As previously identified, each child is unique and what may be considered a reasonable risk for one child may seem terrifying to another. Risk in play should be about engagement, learning and challenge.

Rather than 'planning' opportunities for children to take risks, our role is to create an environment where children choose how to play and how to challenge themselves. Ultimately, children are the ones who can decide what is the *just right challenge* for them.

Dealing with complaints

In my role as Head of School, I have dealt with my fair share of complaints; how we deal with complaints can define our reputation among parents. Complaints can significantly add to workload and stress, especially since the rise of social media. If online complaints become abusive towards members of staff, take screen shots of the material and log the time, date and web address. If the parent refuses to remove the post, contact the social media site to have the content taken down.

Complaint prevention is definitely the best approach. If you are clear about your play ethos and your approach to risk in play, this will limit parental complaints. Make sure your policies are up to date and well understood by staff as well as families. Complaints concerning the safety of a child or staff member obviously need to be dealt with immediately, but, in other cases, don't be afraid to take some time to reflect. Setting a meeting date in the near future can enable all parties to gain perspective. If you have a potentially difficult meeting scheduled, it can be a good idea to have another member of staff or a governor there.

Good relationships and effective communication are key to resolving complaints well. Educational writer, Laura Henry-Allain, suggests that school leaders should 'listen with their heart' (Watkins, 2021). Let parents have their say and show that you want the best for their child. The aim is to arrive at a solution that is acceptable to all, but don't be afraid to remain firm. Dealing with parental complaints can be stressful, time consuming and thankless. Look after yourself and make sure you have support.

Reflective question 12.4

What strategies can we implement to prioritise self-care and seek support to navigate complaints?

Key takeaways

- It is crucial to maintain open and transparent communication with parents to build trust and understanding
- Communicate success stories and positive outcomes to parents and carers to illustrate the benefits of risky play
- Engage parents in the decision-making process to foster a sense of involvement and support
- Consider offering workshops to explain the philosophy and benefits of risk in play
- Ensure a balanced approach to risk in play, respecting each child's unique abilities and comfort levels
- Develop effective strategies for dealing with complaints to maintain a positive relationship with parents.

Part 3
Risky play in practice

This section is all about implementation. Risk assessment is central to enabling children to engage in developmentally healthy play. Obviously, risk management is individual to every setting, but here we offer tips based on research and longstanding experience. As practitioners, there are certain areas that we are often asked about, such as fire and climbing, so we felt it was helpful to explore these in more depth. Rules and boundaries are key to risk management, but how do you ensure children are central to the rule-making and-maintaining process? Within this section, we also discuss observations of risk in play: using *invested watching* and making on-the-spot decisions to ensure a child's safety while also empowering them.

13

Risk assessment

There will of course be situations where the risks outweigh the benefits – but before we all get terrified into banning anything which might possibly cause harm, we need to remember to put the benefits into our risk–benefit assessment.

Newstead, 2016

This chapter

- How safe is safe enough?
- Risk and hazard – what's the difference?
- The benefits of being exposed to hazards

As safe as *necessary*

The title of this section makes clear what we are here to discuss. However, by the end of the section I will have re-titled it. Language matters, and here we will look at this in more detail.

As teachers or practitioners, it is our role to ensure the safety of the children and young people in our care. I suspect that if we were to ask parents what their first priority was when considering those responsible for caring for their children, their child's safety would be the most common response. Indeed, as a parent myself, there is a part of me that wants my child to be 'as safe as possible' at all times, especially if I'm not there! No parent wants their child to be hurt, the very possibility can cause us pain. The temptation is there to wrap them in cotton wool and protect them from everything. But, in the words of Maria, the mother in *My Big Fat Greek Wedding* (2002) (OK, as references go this is different, but stay with me!) – 'I gave you life so you could live it.' As parents we fight that urge to protect against every potential challenge, fall or upset. We know that experiences that challenge our children are those that help them to grow. We know that we have to allow them to make some of their own decisions, even as very young children, in order to learn what they are capable of. When we step back and think more rationally and objectively, we know that the best thing for our children is to be 'as safe as necessary'. So, what is it that is 'necessary' when we assess the potential for risk in our settings, our play spaces and our activities?

Risks and hazards

What we are actually looking at is a balance of two main factors – the risks and the hazards. These are very different things and very easily confused, or rather not separated into distinct characteristics. Let's start with hazards. Put very simply, a hazard is the thing which might cause harm. Considering different environments then, we could make lists of potential hazards. Table 13.1 shows some examples.

Table 13.1 Potential hazards in different environments

Indoor (e.g. classroom)	Public park	Woodland
Wet floor	Litter – glass, drugs equipment	Poisonous plants
Cleaning products	Dog mess	Stinging or biting insects
Glue	Strangers	Child lost/escaped
Open door	Sun	Uneven ground
Sharp objects	Swings	Sticks

Looking at this list your response to each of these issues or items may either be to a) remove the 'thing' (hazard) completely – problem solved; or b) that is 'only a hazard if …' – that is, you can see a way to make it safe(r). What you are doing in that process is weighing up the risk.

A risk is the chance of that hazard actually causing harm. When we first look at our list of hazards, we can give them a score that tells us (and others) how significant the level of risk is if that thing exists in this environment that is being used for this purpose. The scores may look very different for some hazards in a pre-school environment compared with the environment being used by older children. Once we have considered how great the risk is of that hazard causing harm, we can then consider what we might want or need to do about it – these are the mitigating actions that we put in place to make things 'as safe as necessary'. We can then give it another score, to demonstrate that our action has or will make a difference.

Other than ensuring compliance with UK health and safety legislation, how we score doesn't matter, as long as we use a consistent system and demonstrate what the assigned levels mean – for example, colour coding or numbering. Let's have a look at how that might work with the above list of hazards for a group of two- to three-year-olds (see Table 13.2).

Table 13.2 Hazard, risk and management

0 = no risk (hazard eliminated), 1 = low risk, 5 = high risk

Hazard	Risk	Score	Mitigation	New score
Wet floor	Slip/fall	5	Dry the floor/section off to allow to dry	2
Cleaning products	Ingestion or spillage	5	Locked away as per COSHH guidance	0
Glue	Ingestion, on skin	4	Stored out of reach unless used with supervision	1
Open door	Missing child	5	Doors have high opening handles/bars and locks/ catches that children cannot operate	0
Sharp objects	Cuts	4	Remove broken objects, daily check of area	1
Litter – glass, drugs equipment, cigarette butts	Cuts, disease	5	Children taught to identify and tell an adult; adult uses safety gloves to collect and sealed box to remove from site	3
Dog mess	Disease	4	Children taught to identify and tell an adult; adult uses appropriate bag to collect and deposit in nearest bin	3
Strangers	Wandering off, kidnapping	4	Staff alert to other members of the public; high ratios of staff to children for observation, record of children's clothing and appearance before going out	2*
Sun	Burning	4	Children wear hats, long sleeves and sunscreen applied. Limit time in open spaces where there is no shade	1

(Continued)

Table 13.2 (Continued)

Hazard	Risk	Score	Mitigation	New score
Swings and other fixed play equipment	Falls, being hit	3	Adult supervision when using play equipment	2
Poisonous plants	Ingestion, irritation	4	Adults have knowledge of the space and species present, high adult–child ratio, children reminded not to put anything in their mouths except food provided	2
Stinging/biting insects	Irritation, reaction	3	Wear socks, closed shoes and long trousers, check for known allergic reactions, ice packs in first aid kit	2
Keeping children in view	Missing child	5	High adult–child ratio with regular head counts, clear boundaries for the area children stay within, with visual markers	2
Uneven ground	Trips/falls	3	Remind children that the ground may be tricky and to move with care	2
Sticks	Poking injuries	3	Remind children to be aware of tree growth at eye-level in particular, and if playing with sticks to take care to move and carry them safely	2

*may vary in different areas

It is clear from the above examples that some risks are higher than others to begin with and some can be entirely eliminated; it is never OK to put anyone at risk from chemicals or dangerous substances – guidelines exist for that specific example – and serious questions need to be asked of a setting where very young children could open doors and leave. This is very different from the risk of a child going missing in an outdoor environment, as you would automatically have a higher ratio of adults–children if out in a public space and take additional measures to ensure children stay together. Additionally, there are positive reasons for taking children out into different environments. However, that example, like most of the others in Table 13.2, cannot be made risk-free. We cannot guarantee that we can take the level of risk down to zero for most of these hazards.

Reflective questions 13.1

Does everyone in your team have an opportunity to contribute to the list of hazards and potential risks and how to manage them?

Would your team benefit from an opportunity to do this?

Benefits

So, let's have another look at those hazards, and this time let's consider the benefits that being exposed to those hazards might bring to that same group of children aged two to three years. Table 13.3 includes an additional column with a bit more detail or rationale for the benefits.

Table 13.3 Hazard, benefit and rationale

Hazard	Benefit	***Why is it OK?***
Wet floor	Awareness of surroundings	*Level of harm likely minimal*
Cleaning products	None	*Not OK – remove hazard*
Glue	Creative and artistic expression, fine motor skills	*Developing skills and self-esteem*
Open door	None	*Not OK – building should be secure*
Sharp objects	Awareness of surroundings and sense of responsibility	*There may always be something that will accidentally cause a graze or cut*
Litter – glass, drugs equipment, cigarette butts	Awareness of environment, learning to assess risk	*Learning about associated dangers, developing social and environmental responsibility*
Dog mess	Awareness of environment, learning to assess risk	*Learning about dangers, developing social and environmental responsibility*
Strangers	Meeting other people and speaking to members of the public in a group can be positive for community relationships and developing social skills	*Most people are good people, a stranger may just be a friend you haven't met yet; don't want to teach fear. Environment is a resource for all*

(Continued)

Table 13.3 (Continued)

Hazard	Benefit	*Why is it OK?*
Sun	Vitamin D. Children learn about weather and keeping themselves safe in different types of weather	*Adults can manage children's time in the sun based on levels of shade available and children being equipped with hats etc.*
Swings and other fixed play equipment	Developing movement sensations, exploring types of movement	*Children will likely use the playpark with their caregivers at home and/or learn how to manage themselves around the equipment*
Poisonous plants	Connection with nature	*Education about plant life*
Stinging/biting insects	Connection with nature	*Education, respect for other living things*
Keeping children in view	Opportunity for freedom and exploration, develop confidence and self-esteem	*Learning boundaries*
Uneven ground	Develops proprioception, gross motor skills	*Balance and core strength essential for development*
Sticks	Gross and fine motor skills (depending on how sticks are used!), self-esteem	*Awareness of environment and responsibility for own and others' safety*

We can see that the risks associated with children being exposed to these potential hazards can actually have a beneficial learning/development outcome. To remove all hazards completely and keep children in a sterile, risk-free environment would not only be of no benefit, but also it would actively cause a different type of harm by preventing opportunities for learning, for development of key skills and experiences and preventing children from moving freely. In addition, they would not learn about risk and develop the skills to assess risk for themselves and make their own decisions about what felt safe to them.

Reflective questions 13.2

How important do you think it is that we have a rationale for our risky play decisions?

To what extent do your assessments of risk processes communicate this to all stakeholders?

Risk assessment

As previously mentioned, the HSE (2012) states 'the goal is not to eliminate risk, but to weigh up the risks and benefits. No child will learn about risk if they are wrapped up in cotton wool' (p. 1). The concept of risk assessment was originally developed for a workplace environment where there were avoidable hazards that could and should be removed to prevent work-related injury and illness. In the real world, however, in our leisure time and in learning, people need to be able to make their own decisions about the risks they are prepared to take and the trade-off for potential harm. This begins with toddlers deciding when they are ready to pull themselves up against the furniture and take their first steps, continues with the pre-schooler on an adventure playground and deciding whether they dare to walk on the wobbly bridge, or climb a tree or other structure, right through to the skateboarder increasing their skills, the rugby player going in for the hard tackle, etc. In all of these real-world examples, we are firstly (even if subconsciously) concerned with the benefits that pursuing this activity bring – the feelings we get from both daring to try and, hopefully, from succeeding, as well as the skills we develop and the actual achievement. It is a holistic experience that goes beyond the assessment of level of risk, but rather is about our overall well-being. Instead of safety being the priority, we need to look at well-being as the priority. We need to move in ways that challenge us, especially as young children. We need to experience adrenaline and that sense of achievement and exhilaration that only comes from physical challenge (and associated risk).

When talking about the need for a different approach for play and leisure compared to the process of risk assessment for the workplace, David Ball (2007) uses the example of the wobbly bridge – children like to try walking on a wobbly bridge. They actively develop key physical skills through this activity – core strength, proprioception, confidence and self-esteem. Risk is intrinsic to that activity and the wobbly bridge has value and benefits that outweigh the risk. No good can come of a wobbly bridge in a workplace, however.

Benefit–risk assessment

With this in mind, in 2023 a new International Standards Organisation (ISO) standard was published – ISO 4980 *Benefit–Risk Assessment for Sports and Recreational Facilities, Activities and Equipment*. The introduction to this new ISO states:

> The terms 'sports' and 'recreation' describe diverse activities and the necessary equipment for all ages and abilities. It is recognized that sports and recreation involve numerous stakeholders including, but not limited to, designers, manufacturers, installers, owner/operators, maintainers, inspectors of sports and recreation equipment and facilities, and any park rangers, playworkers or activity leaders who may be present at these venues.
>
> ISO, 2023

The ISO is very clearly intended to cover a variety of stakeholders and reflects that a single system of risk assessment for the breadth of sport, recreation and play is not going to be feasible. The key is that sport, recreation and play need a very different approach from that applied in a workplace. Participation in activities or play with an element of risk is recognised as being good for well-being.

> Participation in sport and recreation involves exposure to risk which is not necessarily a bad thing and can be of benefit to the public good. Exposure to risk in daily life can reduce fear and improves the development of human competency, for example, in adventure sports, exposure to risk is what provides part of the enjoyment. Even in the case of children's play provision, it is now widely recognized that children seek risky situations. Graduated challenge provides opportunities for children to develop internal hazard references.
>
> ISO, 2023

The distinction from the workplace is clear, as the benefit–risk analysis demands the consideration of the benefits and the risks into a single evaluation. 'This immediately separates sport and recreation from the world of occupational health and safety where the goal, as noted above, is generally seen as one of eliminating or minimizing risk' (ISO, 2023).

Language

It is extremely significant that the language of this new ISO is deliberately using the word 'benefit' before 'risk'. That sends a very strong message to us all that when we provide opportunities for young people to face risk, we are providing them with a positive and necessary experience. Our responsibility is to ensure that the benefits outweigh the risks so that our children are as safe as necessary, in order for them to enjoy a rich learning and development experience. We are reassured that while injuries can and may happen, that too is a part of learning. As I write this, I am looking forward to a summer of watching the Olympic Games and I know none of these athletes got where they are today without experiencing injury and taking tremendous risks in developing their skills. They are an inspiration to me, and to my young daughter. When she was very little, her inspiration was the slightly older child who could climb to the top of the tree while she was barely able to get up to the first branch – our perspectives change as we grow too!

We began with a title of 'risk assessment'. Now let's focus on shifting our focus and our language, as guided by the ISO, to benefit–risk. Because language matters, as it shapes our whole approach from one guided by fear to one guided by possibility. That's the world I want my children to be growing up in.

Reflective questions 13.3

Is there a 'language of risk' among the adults you work with?

Is it different among parents? How can we help to bring everyone onto the same page?

Case study: risk culture

Megan McGee, Educator, UK

I first became interested in children's risk-taking, including the notion of risky play, after I spent a semester abroad studying in Denmark during my undergraduate degree. There I met with several practitioners, many of whom informed me that it is a part of Danish culture for adults to be 'laid back' concerning children taking risks. I recall fondly a classmate of mine (who also originated from the UK), who had undertaken a placement in a Danish Forest School, tell me the tale of how she had expressed concern over a child (aged no more than five years of age) climbing a tree. She told me that the FS practitioner looked to the child, then back at her, and told her that, 'if he falls, he will know what he did wrong and won't make the same mistake again'. It was one of the first cultural shocks we experienced in those early days in Denmark. Observing children sleeping outdoors in prams was another shock; we couldn't imagine doing such a thing back home in the UK!

During my time in Denmark, I saw students engaging in cooking over an open bonfire. This would be done at least twice a week, where the students would be supervised by a teacher, and everyone would cook a meal together from scratch. Then, they'd gather around the bonfire to eat and talk about their day. At the same location where the cooking activities were held, there was a large shed that held a vast variety of tools which students would use (with permission and guidance from a teacher) to partake in activities such as cooking or craft. Observing this during my placement was quite an experience. My time in Denmark truly altered my perspective of children's risk-taking and that it is something I still carry with me.

(Continued)

Take a moment to reflect upon yourself and your own experiences with children; have you ever been reluctant to initiate an activity with a group of children for fear of the risks it poses?

Key takeaways

- Hazard and risk are different – we can see the hazard but need to understand the risk
- The language of 'risk assessment' was devised for a workplace and does not suit a play environment
- Perspectives on risk are different, depending on the environment, the types of hazard and the potential risk
- In play, we focus on the benefits of the (potentially hazardous) activity and then consider how to reduce the risk
- Language is important – we use benefit–risk assessments in play

14

Areas that are most often asked about

Children love to learn about fire and making fire. So much so that, if they are not facilitated to do so by adults, some will go off and teach themselves about fire, and this is when accidents are more likely to happen.

Holland, 2009

This chapter

- The importance of 'why?' (your rationale)
- Reasons to include tool use with young children
- Getting comfortable with tree-climbing
- Responsible use of fire

The three most frequent areas of interest

When delivering training to Early Years practitioners, there are specific areas of play and learning activities that are asked about more often than others. These are generally climbing trees, using tools and using fire. If we consider everything that we unpicked in the bullet list above and keep in mind the language of benefit–risk, this can be addressed by starting with the simple question 'why?' Simon Sinek (2009) invites us to *Start with Why*. What is your 'why?' for why you are reading this book? Why do you do the job you do? Why do you value the things you do? What is your why? That's a bigger question for way beyond this book! But let's look at the 'why' in relation to these activities, which should naturally lead us to the benefits and then we can carry out our benefit–risk assessment.

Using tools with young children

Using tools is one of my favourite things to do with young children. It is hugely significant in addressing issues of self-esteem, as well as the physical aspects of developing fine motor skills. Tools are so often locked away from children and identified as being 'dangerous' and not for their use ('don't touch!'), that they can develop a great mystery. As we know, nothing makes you want to touch a painted surface like a sign that says, 'wet paint – do not touch'! Why do we want to touch it? Firstly, because we were told not to – there's a rebel in all of us! Secondly, our curiosity gets the better of us. Is it really still wet? We need to check! What

Figure 14.1 Hammering nails into a pumpkin shell

does wet paint feel like? I wonder if my fingerprint will show? As soon as we hear the suggestion that we should not do something, it ignites an insatiable curiosity to know more. For very young children, the concept of danger holds relatively little meaning. They can't visualise the hazard or potential risk. The benefit that they have identified is likely to be around fun and the challenge of touching something they have been told not to. As adults who are aware of the potential actual benefits, we do have a responsibility to reframe the benefits with the children as well as to reduce the excitement factor and to bring the focus to learning and understanding. How we do this will depend on the age of the children, the type of tool we are using and then about the size of the group. These considerations will form our mitigations for reducing the hazards that cannot be eliminated when using tools.

The list of tools which may be used within a childcare or education setting is limitless and will depend entirely on the adults' competence and confidence. I would always recommend specific tools training before starting out with tools; indeed, an insurance company may demand that. You will notice that the trained adult is a feature of the example benefit–risk assessment below. Small hammers may be the easiest tool to introduce though and can be used for a variety of activities throughout the seasons, such as hapa zome, then moving on to hammering nails. Using a pumpkin shell in the autumn can be a great place to start for this, as it is soft and accepts the nails easily, meaning less intense hammering!

With the right training, experience and guidance, children can experience using saws of various types and sizes, cutting tools such as secateurs or loppers (generally older children due to the size and weight of loppers making them more difficult to wield safely), hammers, blades and drills. As well as the learning and developmental benefit, which features on the benefit–risk assessment, we can also look at the wider, practical 'why?' Why this tool? What are we trying to achieve or create? Table 14.1 gives some examples; you will have many more ideas and possibilities appropriate to your settings.

Table 14.1 Tools and suggestions for use

Tool	Project possibilities
Saw (bow saw, folding saw, hacksaw – as appropriate to the size of wood)	Prepare firewood, make crafts – log-dogs, wood cookies, 'gnomes' etc.
Loppers or secateurs (as appropriate to the size of the job)	Conservation tasks – clearing paths, removing trip-hazards (e.g. trailing brambles), craft – trimming sticks or twigs
Hammers	Fixing things, craft – e.g. hapa zome (bashing natural materials between fabric to extract the coloured dyes to create pictures)
Knives (or potato peelers)	Whittling – sticks for toasting marshmallows, increasingly complex crafts as skills develop
Hand drill or palm drill	Bore a hole through a wood cookie

Table 14.2 Benefit–risk assessment example for blades – for example, knives or peelers

Activity	Benefit	Hazard	Risk	Level	Control measures	New level
Whittling with peelers/knives	Self-esteem, confidence, knowledge of keeping safe, sense of achievement Mindfulness – focus on creativity has mental health benefits Remove the mystery and attraction of 'playing' with knives and sharp tools – education	Sharp blades	Cuts / lacerations, serious injury from knife, blood	**High**	Peelers/knives should be kept in good working order and stored in sealed box Tool talk and demonstration before participants allowed to use peelers/knives. Includes information about 'blood bubble', others will be kept away from area where sharp tools are being used. Trained adult supervision for knife use, age-appropriate Safety reminders at the beginning of the session, particularly relating to body position – knives away from thighs Participants should wear a glove on holding (non-dominant) hand if appropriate and use tools in designated area First aid kit containing protective gloves and dressings suitable for bleeding injuries, first aider trained in dealing with bleeds	**Med**

Table 14.2 gives an example of a possible layout of a benefit–risk assessment for one tool from the list. You will see the level of risk given on a scale of high/med/low – no reason, it's just one of the ways you might choose to measure or record level of risk. The benefits are listed first. There is no getting away from the high risk, so the control measures are extensive and detailed, including dealing with injury should it occur.

Reflective questions 14.1

Do you use tools within your setting?

If not, what do you feel you need in order to develop this activity? Who might be able to help?

A similar process to that shown in Table 14.2 should be prepared for each tool that you may use in your sessions. You may wish to differentiate your approach with different groups, perhaps by age, or there may be other variables. Sometimes a 1:1 ratio is the only safe way to proceed, and that would be another control measure. Children as young as two – or possibly even younger, but you will know your children (and parents) to make that decision – can begin to learn about tools, beyond a 'do not touch' approach that does not teach them anything.

Figure 14.2 Child using a hand drill with adult support

Reflective questions 14.2

Would you add anything else to this benefit–risk assessment? Further columns or content?

Would you need to adapt it for your setting or learners?

Case study: woodwork with children

Pete Moorhouse has written comprehensively about using tools with children and works in Early Years settings regularly

Woodwork is a wonderful activity for young children through which they can embrace risk and challenge within a controlled environment. It is so important children are given opportunities to experience risk, allowing them to make their own judgements and decisions. This is an important part of child development. If we deny these opportunities, children are not learning how to risk assess in order to best protect themselves and, subsequently, they will become more susceptible to accidents when they encounter new situations.

Crucial to managing risk is understanding the hazards. With woodwork it is important to take the time to slowly introduce the tools in small groups: learning how to use them safely, discussing the potential hazards and measures we can put in place to reduce these. The HSE emphasises that H&S is really about developing understanding and not blindly following rules (2012). With young children this means having a discussion in a very small group, as there has to be a dialogue to really embed understanding. We should always remember H&S is there to enable activities to be done safely, not prevent them.

It's easy to feel a little apprehensive about woodwork if you have never done it with young children, but, with some very basic H&S measures, we can ensure woodwork is low risk. I've been providing woodwork to young children for over 25 years with no significant injuries. Wearing safety glasses clearly eliminates the chance of eye injury and all the children should absolutely know why they are wearing them and what might happen if they didn't. With hammering it's about learning that once we have tapped in a nail so it's standing on its own, we then need to move our fingers away before hammering hard. We find that behaviour is so often exemplary in the woodwork area as children self-regulate being engaged and focused on something they enjoy doing.

Challenge is also a large part of woodwork. It's actually a pretty awkward material to work with, necessitating constant problem-solving and skill development. It's important not to introduce too much challenge too soon, so children can gradually build confidence, without it being frustrating. It's crucial to allow children the freedom to make what they want to make; that way they have the intrinsic motivation to find their own solutions and, in the process, they will be developing perseverance and resilience.

Risks are further reduced by having the most appropriate tools. For example, 'pull' saws, held with two hands, are much safer for children and short stubby hammers with a large head make hammering so much more controlled. With woodwork there still will be occasional accidents; there will be the odd bruised thumb or even perhaps a small surface cut, but these occurrences are rare and the level of injury is minor. Life inherently contains risk; the important thing is that we learn the skills to navigate this in order to take advantage of the great benefits it offers.

Tree-climbing

Tree-climbing is one of the most fascinating opportunities to facilitate for young children as it offers them so many rich play and learning possibilities. It provides opportunities for children to explore a number of different play types, as well as Sandseter's risky play types (2007) and the *orientation schema*:

- *locomotor play*: physical health and competence, fun and challenge. Includes climbing, jumping and swinging;
- *deep play*: risky experiences with possibility for injury. Provides thrills and exhilaration and opportunity to face and conquer fears;
- *risky play type*: play at height. Reaching a new height, sense of achievement, experiencing great views;
- *orientation schema*: seeing things from a different view. Includes hanging upside-down, looking at from under or above, gaining new perspectives.

Climbing develops strength and balance, challenges the vestibular system and all-round physical abilities. The process of climbing allows for the process of children assessing the risk as they go – checking branches, determining how high is high enough, whether they can still get themselves down. The achieved space and height can be a space of sanctuary – a space to retreat to and just 'be'. Achieving a climbing goal develops confidence and self-esteem.

The *big question* when it comes to climbing (after the 'why?') is how high? The answer, as in many cases, is 'it depends'. On a purely practical and decision-making level, your insurance company may give you a set height. This is commonly 2 metres with the main outdoor learning insurers. Some will offer a variation of up to 5 metres for an additional premium. Managers in a setting may create their own limits (below the insured maximum). For example, no higher than the height of the tallest adult. While there is logic behind this guidance decision, few children can make that assessment while climbing. They may be no more able to accurately assess what 2 metres looks like, but it is definable by a specific point (e.g. a particular branch) and the likelihood is that 2 metres is a realistic climbing height for many Early Years children. It certainly gives them more scope to challenge themselves in a way that is satisfying and genuinely provides challenge and achievement. Another way a 'rule' might be imposed or at least questioned or advised might be by the local authority/HSE/Ofsted/HMIE/Care Inspectorate (depending on where you are). The advent of the new ISO 4980 (2023) hopefully means less curtailing of play with risk and gives practitioners a valuable base to attach rationales to. If you are lucky you will have an inspector like the one I worked with while registering two new settings, who felt that imposing any height restriction at all on tree-climbing was nonsense! That would be reassuring for the setting attended by the daughter of a friend who was somewhat taken aback to find her then-three-year-old rather higher than expected!

Ultimately, much of the decision-making comes down to practitioner knowledge and trust in their relationships with the children. It is important to show that we trust the children and to empower them to listen to their bodies and feelings – sometimes their head will say that's high enough, sometimes it's a feeling of butterflies in the tummy. Rather than telling them how high to go or that they are high enough, ask them to assess the situation for themselves, through their understanding and confidence in their practical skills ('can I get down safely from here?') and through how they feel. These conversations are important in helping them to develop their confidence and trust in their own ability.

If there was one piece of valuable guidance I have learned, as previously discussed, it is to never lift a child up into a tree – it doesn't teach them any skills or develop their abilities in any way, and if they didn't climb up themselves they are unlikely to be able to climb down themselves, or even appreciate how (relatively) high they are. Encourage them to climb something more accessible, or perhaps to problem-solve – could they use a loose/moveable part (tyre, pallet, crate) as a step to help them climb up? Other helpful recommendations for discussions with children include testing the branches before putting full weight on them, and never trying to stand on anything less than the thickness of your wrist. Talk about hazards that may be visible from the ground – your daily grounds assessment (checking your area for hazards before the start of the day, which might include tree damage after high winds, for example) would have identified any obvious loose hanging branches, but you may also be able to identify others not suitable for weight-bearing (too thin), any areas where there may be sharp twigs. It is also worth considering the landing surface; try to ensure the ground is clear of stones or hard/sharp edges as far as possible.

It goes without saying that knowing your children is important when assessing how to provide for risk play experiences such as tree-climbing. I have one particular memory of a child with limited verbal communication who loved to climb and to just lay on a branch and chill. The child was actually a great climber, usually repeated the same climb in the same tree, very happy. On one occasion I saw that they had climbed higher than usual. Still chilling on a branch, looking comfortable. No problem. As they were still there some time later, I went across to see if they were OK. This child was not able to identify their feelings or assess their own capability to get down or not. Fortunately, they did have one appropriate word – 'stuck!' I set about trying to help them down by trying to guide their feet over the branch to then lower down to a point I could reach them better, but so great was their trust in me that they just dropped! Best test my reflexes have ever had!

Reflective questions 14.3

What rules do you have in your setting for certain types of play? Would any of those rules change if a benefit–risk assessment was applied to them?

If you don't have trees in your setting, how do you facilitate climbing opportunities for children?

Learning with fire

This to me is the activity where the question of 'why?' is paramount. This is not only in terms of our own decision-making as adults about whether to have a fire, but also in terms of our communication with children. We have a responsibility to educate around when, where and why it is OK to have a fire. This is perhaps the most important example of an activity where we have to look beyond the learning benefits of undertaking the activity and make the environment our prime consideration. There is more accidental environmental devastation through irresponsible or ill-thought-out use of fire than any other activity, and it is important that this is kept at the forefront of our decisions around this activity. Here the benefits do not always outweigh the risks as they cannot always be sufficiently controlled. In the case of fire, I prefer to take a *responsibility–benefit–risk* approach. The responsibility is to the environment – both the immediate environment (including the direct site of the fire) and the wider environment and community. The primary considerations are:

- local fire-risk level;
- current weather conditions;
- previous/recent weather conditions;
- appropriateness of site;
- equipment.

Most regions across the UK and further afield now have their own fire-risk warnings. These are most often communicated across social media or on web pages, or the local fire service will be happy to advise. Periods of warm, dry weather are a good indicator of an increased risk of wildfires, caused by stray sparks or a fire not fully extinguished. Wind helps to fan flames and feed a fire or smouldering embers. Under or close to lots of trees in a woodland is not usually the best location. We need to consider our impact on the immediate environment even if there is not a heightened risk of wildfires – it's not OK to set a fire on the ground unless this is a prepared, established fire pit, away from any deadwood, tree roots, possible burrows or other wildlife habitat. Fire will always have some impact on the wildlife; we have a responsibility to minimise that. Ideally, we would use a raised fire bowl; certainly, I would argue this when working with children. They will learn what they see, without necessarily taking on board all of the additional considerations of preparations – for example, you may have dug out an area of ground and soaked it with water, you may put the fire out with water and cover the area over in an attempt to 'leave no trace', but underground heat can build, smoulder and restart. Not to mention the underground wildlife that may be disturbed by these actions. Bushcraft survival skills may include making the best of what you have to stay alive, but that's not what we are teaching or needing in this situation. A raised fire bowl is the only responsible way to do fire with young people, unless on a designated site that has established fire pits; where that is the case that fact should be highlighted.

So why a fire? What might the reasons and benefits be? Given the environmental concerns above and other risks (which we will explore shortly) we really need to have a good reason for choosing to include fire in our outdoor learning/play session. These may be:

- warmth;
- focus point;
- heat/cook food or drink;
- learn a skill.

The associated and additional benefits might include:

- comfort;
- safety/security;
- social inclusion;
- health and well-being – warm and nutritious food;
- learning about responsible use of fire, including when it is/is not appropriate to have a fire and where/how to do so, including use of safety equipment;
- risk management;
- sense of achievement, self-esteem and confidence from various responsibilities involved with having a fire, including lighting it;
- resilience;
- other learning opportunities – collecting wood for the fire and choosing what types of sticks/wood to use. This can include measuring and comparing size of twigs/sticks and sorting into size order ready to add to the fire at the right time, as well as what makes good tinder and what will burn for longer.

So, we have justified our 'why?', we have identified the significant benefits; we then need to look at the additional risks, which are the risks to participants. These are primarily:

- burns or scalds – sparks from the fire or touching the fire or equipment;
- smoke inhalation – wind blowing smoke, getting too close;
- fire spreading – fire made too big for the purpose;
- fire not completely extinguished – failing to check properly and leave enough time.

As with tools, one of our control measures would be to have a suitably trained member of staff – in both the use of fire and in associated first aid if needed. Recommended guidance is available through Outdoor Woodland Learning Scotland (OWLS, 2024), but this should not be used in place of training, rather to supplement the correct training. There was an incident of a child burned by incorrect use of a camping kettle a number of years ago. The OWL fire guidance was held up as example of good practice to follow.

Reflective questions 14.4

What are the benefits that you have seen from introducing fire with a group?

Have you ever experienced a situation where the challenges have been so significant that they appeared to outweigh the benefits? If so, how have you overcome this?

Case study: burns from a fire

An account from a parent whose child was burned after using a barbeque on the beach and believing they were doing everything safely.

After a beautiful evening and barbeque at Yellowcraigs, we cooled the already-cooling-fast disposable barbecue with water. When we picked it up a few mins later, it was cool enough to lift comfortably in bare hands and even the underside felt only warm (admittedly I only felt it near the edge). A few minutes later [my daughter] was screaming like I'd never heard her before. I couldn't get out of her what was wrong and thought she must have been stung by something. But when I looked under her foot, I saw burns. She had stood in the patch of sand that had been under the barbecue. I maybe should have clocked that the sand would retain so much heat and at such a high temperature, but I didn't.

The next hour was horrendous, with continual screaming and crying as I cooled her foot in the sea, carried her to the car park and drove to A&E. Thankfully it was superficial and healed fine.

This incident highlights two important considerations – the human safety element that ultimately resulted in this injury, and the environmental element that the residual heat from this barbecue being placed directly on the ground was immense, and far greater than the family had assumed. They acted responsibly in every way they knew, actively cooled the area (as far as they were aware), but the effects of the heat in the ground was not something they were aware of. They are not alone, and this is not something that it is easy to find education on. It is rarely highlighted in any form of bonfire or barbecue education. If it was, this injury might have been prevented. In a different environment, the same scenario could cause extensive environmental damage.

Key takeaways

- Using tools, climbing trees and using fire are the areas of risky play or activity that are most frequently asked about and that do have the greatest potential for injury
- Know your 'why' for including these in your setting
- These areas usually require specific insurances to be in place
- Staff being appropriately trained is a mitigating factor that reduces risk

15

Observation and adaptation

I now try to follow the 17-second rule before I step in when I see risky play going on. It's been a process!

Jayne, Nursery Teacher

This chapter

- The importance of observing children taking risks in play
- The concept of invested watching
- The value of giving children time for self-directed play
- The principles of dynamic risk assessment
- The significance of reflective practice in supporting children's development and managing risk in play
- Closely observing children's play to give us crucial insights into their development and next steps
- Invested watching, requiring us to be fully present and attentive to build the relationship
- The value in enabling children to have prolonged periods of self-directed play – this helps us see patterns in play
- Making on-the-spot decisions about risk during outdoor play, ensuring children's safety while also empowering them
- Reflecting on and discussing observations with colleagues, parents and the children themselves to enhance understanding and help us to avoid bias

Invested watching

It is only when adults step back (while observing closely) that we can be surprised.

Anji Play, n.d.

What I call *invested watching* of children's play gives us the insights we need to help children progress. This is especially important for very young children or children who have issues with communication. If, like me, you often have an iPad to hand when outdoors, I'm sure you will also find yourself putting it down while observing play with risk so that you can be completely present. It's the type of play where we need to be calm, attentive and in the moment. We are sharing a moment that is thrilling, exhilarating and scary. Being aware of any biases we might have helps us to put these to one side as we observe, so we remain open-minded and curious.

Reflective question 15.1

Reflecting on our own biases, how can we ensure that they do not interfere with our ability to observe children's play objectively and with an open mind?

Time

I couldn't do it then I did do it! I tried and tried. I started the fire in the shell!

William, 5

Time is a thread that runs through this book. Children need prolonged periods of self-directed play and multiple opportunities to play in risky ways. Having the time to watch children play in challenging ways in different contexts can help us see patterns of behaviour and decide on how to support them. Repeated patterns of behaviour or schemas give us insights into the way children think. For example, as a newly qualified teacher, I felt exasperated by a child who was constantly throwing stones outside. He was very upset when a stone hit another child, but carried on throwing stones the next day. Observing his play more closely, I saw that he was transfixed by how high different objects would travel when thrown in the same way. I worked with him to find a range of objects to compare such as foam balls, beanbags and tennis balls. We also talked about the best areas where he could throw these. Observing a child taking risks in different contexts gives us a good picture of who the child is and what taking a risk means to them.

Thanks to funding from a charity called George's Fund (n.d.), I was able to work outdoors over a number of months with a small group of children who had experienced trauma. One girl seemed fearless. She climbed trees, jumped from high log stumps and was confident using tools. After a few weeks, I noticed that she always spent a few minutes watching other children swinging in the hammock. I asked if she'd like to try it, but she laughed and ran away. One week, she touched the fabric and then quickly moved away again. The following week I asked if she'd like to put one of the soft toys in the hammock. She carefully put an owl into the hammock and swung it, saying 'Not too high … not too high …' When someone else tried to join her in pushing the owl, she became angry. A few weeks later, she felt confident to go in the hammock, insisting that only I should push her. I initially thought that she was not interested in hammock play, but observations over time showed me that this was something that was emotionally challenging for her. It's useful to see children taking risks in different contexts, including expeditions outside the setting. It can help build a holistic picture of a child to see images and videos of play sent in by parents and carers.

Reflective question 15.2

Considering the value of observing children taking risks in various contexts, how can we incorporate opportunities for outdoor expeditions?

Planning next steps

Observing risk in play helps us understand what interests and motivates a child and what, if any, level of support a child needs from us. Do we need to intervene or step back? Many children are drawn to building high towers. We might see a child trying to lift a cable reel onto the top of a stack of other cable reels and we could suggest ways to make this structure more stable and accessible. The child in this case may welcome our intervention as a taller person!

If we see that a child is struggling emotionally, we may need to adapt the activity and make it easier to access. For example, I recall seeing a child at the front of a long queue for the rope swing, standing still and crying. Some children were trying to comfort him, others were berating him. I pulled over a log stump so that he could stand on this and more easily access the swing. Once he was safely on the swing, I was able to pull the log stump away. I brought it back when he was ready to get off.

Our observations can help us extend children's play, drawing on their interests. When activities have an element of risk, boundaries may need to be explained. For example, one of my pupils was transfixed by trying hapa zome, or leaf bashing. During the next session,

I provided the same hammers plus scrap wood, nails and safety goggles. I supported her to plan and carry out woodwork projects and she was then keen to take some hammers to a different part of the outdoor area to use in role play. We discussed the fact that the hammers must always stay in the woodworking area but that sticks could be used to take their place, acting as hammers.

Figure 15.1 Drawing on children's interests

> **Reflective question 15.3**
>
> How do we determine when intervention is necessary and when it's appropriate to step back and allow children to explore their boundaries?

Dynamic risk assessment

He was riding his bike, but we was drawing there. It was the same place. Amelie was angry, she got scared. I said, 'You have to go round. Amelie could get hurt.' He went to another bit.

Alessandra, 5

In our observations of outdoor play, we are continually looking for the subtle nuances that tell us that things are becoming dangerous, physically or emotionally. Early Years practitioners are skilled at noticing when there is a change, when a child or group of children seem less safe. There can be a moment when things seem out of control, and we have to decide what action to take.

This is *Dynamic Risk Assessment*, where we make on-the-spot decisions about risk as we watch outdoor play. Dr Mariana Brussoni talks about the 'lifeguard approach' (Gill et al., 2019) where we don't intervene unless someone is really at risk of harm. Here are the three suggested stages, drawing on the idea of 'vigilant care' suggested by Dr Haim Omer (2017):

1. *open observation*: at this stage, we can play alongside the children, trusting children to manage the level of risk in their play. We express caring interest. We can take a non-intrusive approach and avoid interfering if not needed. This is where we should operate most of the time;
2. *focused attention*: when we start to perceive early warning signs of danger, we get closer and check in with the children to check if they are aware of the risk and if they feel comfortable managing it. Dialogue is crucial here. If the children feel they can manage the risk, we can go back to open observation;
3. *active intervention or active protection*: when the level of risk becomes unacceptable to us, we intervene and make an immediate change, taking steps to reduce the level of risk. Even so, we ensure our language is still empowering to the children rather than making them feel powerless. The goal is to give them a better understanding of managing risk and increased confidence. This approach helps us to avoid interfering if not necessary, but act decisively if we see clear signs of danger.

Reflective question 15.4

How do we cultivate a supportive environment where children feel empowered to manage risk while also being responsive to their needs when intervention becomes necessary?

Sharing observations

The child should be at the centre of our thinking with observations; it can be productive to share recordings of adventurous play with the children who feature in them. Children can provide important context that we might be missing and also reflect on what happened.

As part of our reflective practice, discussing observations of risk in play with colleagues can give a different context and avoid our own biases having an impact. Sharing our observations of adventurous play with parents and carers can strengthen the message about the benefit of risk in play, as well as building a link between home and the setting.

Case study: Melissa Littlestone, Twiggles Explorers Forest School and Outdoor Play

I run a well-established after-school club where some children have been attending for between two to four plus years. Only just this week, I could see my group of Year 5 boys, with some new attendees from their class, poised with large knobbly sticks overhead and others pointing in faces. One boy was kneeling down, holding a stick between each hand while another was poised, with his stick touching it in the middle. They were all talking pleasantly and at times excitedly and all were stood like statues, apart from the other observers. I wanted to ensure the two new attendees knew of our group agreement around sticks and their imaginary play wasn't going to turn into a trip to the hospital. I took a slow casual walk over to them and asked them, casually and non-judgementally, if they had explained to the new attendees how we hold sticks and what we do when in 'combat'. (Stick to stick contact only, no pointing in faces or touching bodies, always ensure you can see both ends of your stick etc.).

One of the boys reeled the rules off straight away and another told me what they were doing. I very casually said, 'OK, as long as no one loses an eye, or gets hurt because that's what was worrying me. Cool, OK, carry on!' And I casually walked away. I carried on observing from afar for a minute or two (nobody was looking my way) until I was happy that I did indeed fully trust what they had said. I tend to keep what I say to them very simple and short (not lecturing or complaining) because I know that they're going to get bored or think I'm nagging if it's too long-winded. I might just need them to know that I'm worried or scared (again using humour – worst-case scenario), and seeking their assurance.

It's about really knowing your children and their characters and them knowing that you trust them, with a bit of added humour. Have children ever got hurt during stick combat? Maybe once, nothing serious, but it hasn't happened since and rarely at all because these children have been given the freedom to play with sticks in the first place. They are the experts of stick play!

I think most class teaching staff would baulk at what I allow children to do and would probably give me a shocked or possibly disapproving look or even tell the children off if they saw some of the things I let them do. These children know I trust them, and I trust what they tell me when they explain what they are doing – 99 per cent of the time! In this example of risky stick play, they had assessed the risks for themselves. While they had broken some boundaries (raising a large stick above their heads in close proximity to a friend), the intention was not to hit, but to pose, like a figurine, in battle.

Risky play for me is about giving children the tools (or rules/group agreement) to be safe, observing from a distance without stepping in, stepping in calmly and casually if you feel concerned and continuing to build and maintain mutual trust and respect between you and the children with honesty and humour and by showing your approval. Nobody got hurt that evening and nobody lost an eye! If I were to sum up the process of building mutual trust with regards to risky play it would be this:

1. observe from afar;
2. check in with them in a relaxed manner, explain your concern/worries if you have them;
3. are the rules being enforced; can they tell/demonstrate to you what they are?
4. show/give them your approval;
5. sneakily observe from afar;
6. smile smugly about how much you love these children because they are so ace.

I think it's so important that we show we trust children and that they can trust us.

Key takeaways

- Observing children in different contexts, including outdoor expeditions, helps build a more comprehensive picture of their development and risk-taking behaviours
- Creating a supportive environment where children feel empowered to manage risks is crucial for their confidence and learning
- Knowing when to intervene and when to step back is essential for fostering children's independence and problem-solving skills
- Building mutual trust through honest communication enhances the effectiveness of risk management in play
- Reflecting on our biases, intervention strategies and the value of risky play helps improve our practices and supports children's growth

16

Rules and boundaries

Really, you want this to be a collaborative approach where you explain and negotiate with the children a simple charter or rule set that you all agree to follow with clear justifications for each point.

Bottrill, 2018

This chapter

- Rules and boundaries are necessary in some situations
- How we can ensure everyone contributes to the decisions about what the rules should be
- Thinking about how to best involve the children in these decisions

Who decides on the rules and boundaries in your setting?

As a society, we have moved a long way from the way children used to be viewed – 'children should be seen and not heard', as my grandparents' generation might have said. We now understand so much more about children's competence and we value their contributions. Article 12 of the United Nations Convention on the Rights of the Child (1989) is about respecting children's views.

> Every child has the right to express their views, feelings and wishes in all matters affecting them, and to have their views considered and taken seriously. This right applies at all times, for example during immigration proceedings, housing decisions or the child's day-to-day homelife.

The importance of the child's voice is recognised and highlighted throughout the UK and in increasingly more countries worldwide. In England and Wales, *Birth to 5 Matters* (EYC, 2021, p. 9) tells us that:

> Listening to children and recognising their voices are expressed in a range of ways, including non-verbally, is central to inclusive practice. Children's right to be heard and have their views taken seriously was established via Article 12 [of the UNCRC] and is embedded in the statutory provisions in England of the Special Educational Needs and Disability Code of Practice: 0 to 25 years (DfE/DoH, 2015). Through the Code of Practice, local authorities are mandated to ensure that children's and families views are sought and contribute to educational decision-making.

Giving children a voice in Early Years education can help them feel valued and important, and can also support their learning and development:

- *self esteem*: children can learn that their opinions, feelings and emotions matter, and that they are respected and listened to. This can help boost their self-esteem and self-worth;
- *independent thinking*: when children are encouraged to share their ideas with supportive adults, they can develop independent thinking skills;
- *engagement*: children can feel more meaningfully engaged with their learning and decision-making processes when their voices are heard. This can lead to more successful plans that focus on their interests and needs;
- *sense of belonging*; actively listening to children can help them feel important and that what they say is significant. This can strengthen their bond with adults and others and help them develop a sense of belonging and confidence.

If we consider all of this in the context of benefit–risk management and assessment, what do we actually mean? Are we happy for children to conduct their own assessments and decide on their own sets of rules or boundaries for if or how an activity should happen? Some adults might meet that suggestion with horror and see wild irresponsibility and ridiculousness, and I would absolutely understand where they were coming from. But if we all stepped back and considered the wider picture, we might agree on the ideal scenario being somewhere in between.

Reflective question 16.1

How far do children get to contribute to decision-making and rules in your setting?

Involving young children in decisions

Young children struggle with impulse control; this is the first thing I think of when I consider their ability to form any sort of decision about how to manage risk. They are very likely to want to touch the sharp things, investigate the hot burny things and eat the shiny juicy things, above any other potential play opportunities. As adults with experience of managing expectations and persuading others to our way of thinking, we know that the best way to get someone to do what we would like them to do is to make them think it was their idea in the first place. It is therefore up to us to frame the sharp/hot/juicy things in a way that says, 'Wouldn't be great if we knew more about these so we know how to enjoy them safely?' and get children to come on that journey of discovery and learning with us. If we share with children the benefits of taking part in a suggested activity, this shows them that we are on their side, we want them to be able to do the thing they want to do. If we then highlight some of the hazards associated with that activity (with a little suggestion the children may be able to identify these for themselves), the children will most likely be able to come up with the risks. The sense of responsibility they will feel from this alone will give them a considerable sense of achievement and self-worth. Their understanding, emerging knowledge and views are important, their questions lead to discussion and answers. Finally, armed with their new understanding of hazards and risks, they can be invited to come up with suitable control measures – how can they help to keep themselves and others safe?

In *Outdoor Learning Across the Curriculum* (Beames et al., 2024, p. 130) it is stated that:

> A risk assessment, in particular, should not be something that is 'done' to a group of young people; they need to play a strong role in identifying substantial and foreseeable hazards they might encounter, and in devising strategies to minimise the likelihood of being harmed by them.

Dynamic risk assessments

Beames et al. (2024) are primarily talking about groups of older students, but do go on to identify that with younger children this might take the form of a more dynamic risk assessment approach, where the risks are assessed as hazards emerge throughout the learning experience. They also clarify that the official documentation (our benefit–risk assessments as discussed earlier in this chapter) has already been completed by the group leader. It would appear then that the children are not really contributing their views – the leader is merely paying lip-service to the idea of children having a voice. It could be argued that it would be a very egotistical and closed-minded leader who would not add in to their original benefit–risk assessment the observations and ideas of the children as they emerge. A benefit–risk should be a working document, and benefit-risk assessment should always be a feature. A change in the weather immediately alters both the benefits of an activity and the level of risk from certain hazards (e.g. trees become more slippery to climb safely when wet, fire risks increase with warm, dry weather and wind, etc.). A change in the numbers of children present, which children are present or absent, which combinations of children are present, a new (to the children) environment – these things all impact the activity. The adults will be 'reading' their group in deciding whether an activity goes ahead or with what parameters in place. And here lies the bottom line – the group leader is ultimately and legally the one in charge and has the final say in any decision-making. But if we value the children's input, rather than the answer to 'can we ...?' being 'no', if it needs to be 'no' it will be either 'no, because ...', or, even better where possible, 'what do you think?' The more we can bring the journey to the solution back to the children, the further we are on the path to helping them to become responsible citizens, confident individuals, effective contributors and successful learners (Scottish Executive, 2004, p. 3).

Reflective questions 16.2

How often are your existing benefit–risk assessment documents amended during the course of a day?

How is your dynamic assessment of changes recorded?

Children's voice

Johann Christoph Arnold (2014) highlights some of the ways society treats children. One of his criticisms is when we, as adults, view children as mini-adults, expected to understand our views and expectations.

> And the best antidote to that is to drop all of our adult expectations entirely, to get down on the same level as our children, to look them in the eye. Only then will we begin to hear what they are saying, to find out what they are thinking, and to see ... their point of view.
>
> p. 42

Alison Clark's *mosaic* approach gives important and fascinating insights into how we might best seek the children's voice, reminding us that non-verbal messages hold just as much weight as more clearly articulated language and giving lots of suggestions as to how we can capture that. Her books are well worth looking at for further reading around this area.

> The phrase 'voice of the child' may suggest the transmission of ideas only through words, but listening to young children, including pre-verbal children, needs to be a process that is open to the many creative ways young children used to express their views and experiences.
>
> Clark, 2017, p. 24

So back to the original question – who decides the rules and boundaries in your setting? In addition, are children able to formulate rules? Are they able to question the rules? Are they actively encouraged to do either? It would be really easy to have the adults decide this is the way it is and share that with the children. We can do that gently and in a sharing manner rather than dictatorial finger-wagging, but let us not pretend that means we are listening. Article 12 of the UNCRC (1989) is clear – even if it is not enshrined in law throughout the whole of the UK (yet!) – in matters affecting them, which includes decisions about their play, they have a right for their voices to be heard. That includes the right to question, to negotiate, to understand. Their safety does ultimately mean that some things are non-negotiable. But if they are not able to ask the question, they may not be able to understand. If we don't allow them to contribute, we cannot learn from their understanding and viewpoint. UNICEF's *Rights Respecting Schools* is an initiative which encourages this in all schools; many are taking it forward (UNICEF, 2024).

A fascinating study took place in Verona, Italy, where practitioners gave nursery children the opportunity to plan, develop and lead an 'adventure' project around their local area. Adventures included cave exploration, orienteering in woods, free exploration of natural space, an adventure in the dark and adventures involving climbing – trees and rocks, with and without ropes and specialist instruction. The ideas, and research, for the project initially came from observations of children's play and shared stories and conversations, but the key factor that sets this project apart is that the research, planning and leading of the project was all with the children. The skill of the practitioners lies in their questioning and managing of reflective discussion to facilitate the children finding the solutions and best ways for themselves. The project was completely experiential, so lots of learning took place in real, in-the-moment active experiences, involving test and challenge. 'We now observe that these children display increased autonomy and have more faith in their abilities. They take personal initiatives with ease, even if a great deal of ability is required to ensure that set rules are followed' (Mortari and Zerbato, 2007/8, p. 69).

A local primary school had a playground rule about where balls should be used, with the intention to reduce risk for those not involved in the ball play. A group of boys found a stray ball and came up with a game against a wall. They knew their game was at risk as it technically broke the rules. They approached the playground supervisor and highlighted their understanding of the hazards and risk and explained their control measures, promised to remain only in a designated area and negotiated a deal – if they kept to their control measures and there were no issues, their game could continue. Any issues, however, and it was actual game over. Their game continued every playtime for the rest of the year. Now we are dealing with Early Years, and these were primary school children with a slightly more developed sense of awareness and the language to communicate. But the point is the same – children will rise to the occasion if allowed to, they will grow in confidence if trusted and they will (usually) repay that trust with responsibility. Don't all of our children deserve that opportunity?

Reflective question 16.3

Considering that children in the Early Years may be pre-verbal or, in the case of the younger children, have limited verbal communication skills, how can we still ensure that their voice is heard?

Key takeaways

- Children's rights include the right to be involved in decision-making where it affects them or their play
- Assessing risk is a dynamic process and regular changes or amendments may need to be made
- Benefit–risk assessments are working documents
- Children's voice is imperative – for us to fulfil our duty in terms of children's rights and to help them feel valued and to work with us
- Very young children can be leaders if adults can facilitate skilfully

17

Why does discrimination in play matter?

Risky play is an effective route to fun and learning. The power for Clem to be in charge of her own fun, decision-making and control within her limitations. If you can bring that out of someone and really develop it, it's life enhancing, a life source and well … everything really.

Vicky Nicolson-James

This chapter

- Children learn and face challenges differently, requiring tailored support
- The importance of providing equitable play opportunities for all children, including those with disabilities
- How gender stereotypes influence children's play and how to challenge these stereotypes
- Ways to create inclusive play environments that accommodate children of all abilities and backgrounds
- The role of reflective practice in identifying and addressing biases

Inclusivity in play

Children are not robots. They learn in different ways and at different paces. A challenge in a natural environment will be completely different for two different children. It might be climbing a tree for one child, whereas for another child it could be allowing a woodlouse to crawl on their hand. Young children instinctively need to repeat things over and over again to master them and become confident and playful, but unfortunately the time they need for this mastery stage is sometimes curtailed.

We know through research that age, gender and disability status has an impact on how thoroughly a child can engage in play that challenges them (Dodd et al., 2021). There are factors that can make children more vulnerable, such as reduced communication or mobility issues. Children sometimes need additional support to tackle obstacles and solve problems, but the research indicates that children with SEND are often overly limited by adults in their play.

Case study: making people think differently

Vicky Nicolson-James, a therapist specialising in hypnotherapy, NLP, EFT, psychotherapy and emotional support, based in Herefordshire

My middle child is Clementine, who's 20; she has multiple disabilities. Sensory play has been really important from the moment she was born. Clem's diagnosis is agenesis of the corpus callosum, which means she's got a lack of cabling from left to right and right to left. The corpus callosum just didn't form when she was in uterine. We were told we had to 'install' as much information as possible as she would have severe learning difficulties as a result. Clem's optic nerve also wasn't developed properly. So visual input also needed to be installed as much as we could. From the very beginning sensory play has been important so that Clem could take on board as much learning and fun as she could.

It takes Clem's brain a long time to register what's happening, but once she gets it, she really gets it. She used to love throwing things on the floor that would clatter. She kind of led us down the risky play route herself. For example, the only thing she could do was roll when she was little (she can't do it now, but she could at the time). She went to nursery at Barons Cross, Leominster, and we had this brilliant practitioner there who did sports. She said, 'Right, Clem can only roll. She can't run, kids. We're all going to have a rolling race.' It was great. And she won. And I was so proud of her because she won a sports race. She just brought it to Clem's level. It was genius.

So rolling was a big thing when Clemmy was little. She used to roll off the sofa into my arms and she would just laugh her head off. And it would go on for hours. My arms would be aching, but it was something that she had

(Continued)

control of. And she could initiate it. You know, she'd try and roll off anything and she'd look at you with this mischievous look: 'Come on, we're playing this game!' I was kind of led by her on that. She can't talk. She can't do anything in a typical kind of way. But she could roll. There was a massive step in the kitchen, and she used to roll down it and laugh her head off. We'd all go: 'Don't roll!' And then she'd roll towards the dishwasher, open the dishwasher and just play with the dishwasher door. Any social worker or new health professional would say: 'Oh my God!' and they ended up making her wear a hard hat. Clem was such a risk-taker, but she loved it because she was free, and she instigated it and she had control over it. We had so many people trying to input onto her, which was great, but it was so forced. They were only trying to do their best. Take the visual impairment people, for example; they were trying to test where her vision is and she only had peripheral vision. They were saying 'Clem, look at this. Look at this!' She's quite a monkey, and the pressure was on for her to perform, and she wouldn't do it. I get that they haven't got the experience that I've got, but I said, 'If you do it this way, you'll get a much better result.' And sure enough, she would do it. She'd do it because she was caught unawares. She was in control, and she was the boss. And it was not forced on her.

There is that saying isn't there? I'm not disabled. It's my environment that disables me. And it's so true. What we're aiming to do is not be judgemental, but to say, 'Have you thought of …?' It's different approaches. Just making people think differently.

Giving enough time for understanding and reaction is important. I have to give Clem time because it takes about a minute for it to get all the way around her brain. Then for her to understand what's happening, it can take a long, long time. I have a video, filmed at Queenswood; it's my youngest pulling the branches of the beautiful red maple tree in the autumn garden and Clem is in her wheelchair underneath. My youngest is shaking it and shaking it for ages and ages and ages. And the leaves are falling on Clem, and there's no reaction. And then as soon as I stopped filming, she started to giggle. I was like, 'God, I didn't capture the giggle!' Because it took that long for the reaction, for her to take on board what was being done and for her to react.

Risky play is an effective route to fun and learning. The power for Clem to be in charge of her own fun, decision-making and control within her limitations. If you can bring that out of someone and really develop it, it's life enhancing, a life source and well … everything really.

Reflective question 17.1

How do we adapt our support strategies to ensure all children have equitable opportunities to engage in risk in play?

Gender and risk in play

> *No one part of society can make the change needed when it comes to gender stereotypes – we all have to pull together. Unless we all do so, each of us will fear that changes they make in one area will be overridden elsewhere.*
>
> Fawcett Society, 2020

Figure 17.1 Building identity through play

Children start to build their identity and explore gender through play. Whether we are aware of it or not, we send out messages about gender roles and expectations, and we need to be aware of social expectations that can limit children's choices based on their gender. For example, boys can often be encouraged to take part in more adventurous and risky play. The pressure can come from peers as well as adults. Both boys and girls need opportunities to challenge themselves in their play.

I'm sure we have all had occasions where we have challenged attitudes from children such as:

- that pink material is just for girls;
- boys are better at climbing trees;
- girls are worse at throwing.

Sometimes, we have to work against unhelpful beliefs that children have internalised and actively challenge gender stereotypes by discussing with children the idea that certain activities or behaviours are not limited to one gender. Part of our role is to encourage children to question stereotypes.

Research shows that by the age of around 18 months, children use gender labels and, interestingly, girls use gender labels earlier than boys, even when adjusting for general language development (Martin and Ruble, 2010). A study by Dr Helen Dodd et al. (2021) found that parents of boys encouraged their child's involvement in risky play and perceived less need to safeguard them from potential injuries than parents of girls. Previous studies have suggested that caregivers are more tolerant of risk in play for boys (Morrongiello et al., 2010). Dodd's research established striking parent gender differences for specific types of risky play activities, and this was particularly true for very high-risk activities. Fathers expressed much higher tolerance of activities such as letting the child play near steep cliffs, playing in the woods out of sight and climbing up a rock wall, irrespective of child gender.

Through months of research and evidence-gathering, the Fawcett Society (2020) found that gender stereotypes can significantly limit children as they grow up, contributing to mental health issues, low self-esteem, body-image issues, higher male suicide rates and violence against women and girls. Their findings are that gender stereotypes continue to be widespread and deeply embedded and that significant changes are needed in education.

We know that gender stereotypes dictating what is acceptable for boys or girls start early. A survey by Girlguiding UK found that more than a third of seven- to ten-year-old girls believe women are rated more on their appearance than their abilities (Topping, 2016). Feeling pressure to stay neat and clean can limit adventurous play, and girls are more likely to be praised for being tidy.

As educators, it's our role to challenge gender stereotypes and be aware of the female-dominated nature of our profession. However, gender is an increasingly emotive issue that arouses strong emotions; this can make people anxious about venturing into this area. As with all areas of justice and equality, children tend to be tolerant of diversity unless they learn intolerant views. Risk in play can be a good way to enable non-gendered play. Natural environments, on the one hand, can be less *gender-coded* and prompt more collaborative play between girls and boys (Änggård, 2011). Indoor environments, on the other hand, can sometimes silently convey gender-specific codes.

Loose parts are generally genderless. For example, lengths of fabric can be more inclusive than dressing-up clothes. However, sometimes adults can imbue loose parts play with their own gendered thinking. A child who is constructing an obstacle course from cable reels and planks might feel she needs to adapt her play if an adult asks: 'Are you building a kitchen?' As well as our language, we can model gender-inclusive behaviour through our actions. As a Forest School leader, I use tools such as drills and knives with children. I sometimes find that girls are initially more hesitant to use tools, but feel a huge sense of accomplishment when they use them successfully. We can model non-stereotypical behaviour in our outdoor play, particularly in our role play. When children can play in an outdoor environment that encourages exploration and experimentation and provides opportunities to play in different ways, this can help avoid gendered play. If all children can choose to climb, build and explore nature, gender becomes less of an issue.

Risk in play often prompts cooperative play that transcends gender stereotypes. Group activities and collaborative projects using loose parts provide opportunities for children to each contribute their own skills, regardless of gender. For example, I was recently working with a group of Reception children who found a pile of long sticks. They decided to build a bridge and worked together to make it strong enough to hold their weight. Roles were assigned among the team simply according to their skills and enthusiasm.

Reflective question 17.2

How can we initiate staff discussions around gender inclusivity, fostering a culture of respect and equality?

Disability

> *For children with disabilities, free risky play is even more crucial than for their peers without disabilities, but they often face major barriers (e.g. lack of accessible playgrounds, overprotective attitude of caregivers) that can prevent them from fully benefiting from the opportunities afforded by this kind of play experience.*
>
> Francesca Caprino, 2018

Enabling all children to fully participate in outdoor play and providing equitable play opportunities means recognising that every child is different and needs varying levels of support. Children with SEN are often unnecessarily restricted from taking part in adventurous play (Caprino, 2018). Many children with disabilities become used to having things done for them and experience less freedom of choice. As Sanders points out (2006), lowered expectations and overprotection are forms of discrimination and internalisation of this discrimination can make a child feel they are less capable. Risk in play is an opportunity to build trust and raise expectations.

Adult concerns about safety can limit access to risky play, but social and environmental factors also play a part. The social model of disability, developed by disabled people, proposes that people are disabled by physical or attitudinal barriers in society, not by their impairment (Shakespeare, 2004). It is important to be aware of barriers that make it difficult for children to access risk, without over protecting them. When we remove these barriers, it opens up more independence, choice and control. To reduce barriers, we can assess the space in terms of *universal design*, which aims to make things accessible to everyone without the need for adaptations or specialised designs (Lynch et al., 2018).

Table 17.1 Universal design principles

Principle 1	Equitable use	The play space is accessible and appealing to all and no children are stigmatised or segregated
Principle 2	Flexibility in use	Children with a wide range of individual preferences and abilities can participate
Principle 3	Simple and intuitive use	Regardless of experience, knowledge, language skills, or education level, the play space makes sense
Principle 4	Perceptible information	The children using the play space understand everything they need to
Principle 5	Tolerance of error	Hazards are minimised
Principle 6	Low physical effort	The play space can be used effectively and comfortably with a minimum of fatigue

For every child, risk in play is individual. It's about the sense of achievement they feel after completing a challenge. It's about the belief that all children, regardless of ability, can benefit from and contribute to risky play. For children with additional needs, choice can be even more important.

Reflective question 17.3

How can we challenge societal attitudes and environmental barriers that restrict children with disabilities from engaging in risky play?

Case study: Marches Family Network

Meg Chambers, Projects Coordinator and Leader. The network provides high-quality, inclusive short breaks for children and young people with disabilities

Risky play is a vital aspect of play for all children. Disabled children are no different, and they should be encouraged to take part in risky play, just as their peers are. Unfortunately, not many spaces are truly accessible. That's where spaces such as Marches Family Network come in. Truly accessible sessions for all young people, regardless of their disability – space for them to play and be themselves and be encouraged to take part in a wide variety of different activities.

Recently, we have been taking part in Forest School sessions with a range of different providers. There have been two clear favourite activities the children have taken part in – cooking on a fire and using hand tools. Parents and carers are always shocked when they are shown and told what their young person has been up to at the session. They struggle to believe that their young person has been allowed to use the tools or been trusted around a naked flame. The shock is even higher when we tell them that it was their young person who actually started the fire!

A lot of people, including parents and professionals, underestimate what their child can truly do and achieve. If we allow children to continue playing the same way with no change, and no risk, how can we expect them to learn and develop? We have one child that has attended our sessions now for many years. He has a diagnosis of ASD and is non-verbal – often resulting in people underestimating his abilities. He always enjoys trying new things and seeing his friends at our sessions. One day, we sat him down with a hand-held drill, offering him the chance to make a medal. His smile lit up the room, as he independently drilled a hole into the wood.

Through risky play, children can continue to acquire new skills. This constant development is crucial in order to encourage independence and learning of life skills.

Racism and risky play

When we talk about play, we need to think about the myth of misbehaviour for Black boys, and the over-policing of the Black child and the restricting of play. Black boys are policed in the nursery environment, the school environment and within wider society.

Liz Pemberton, n.d.

As in other areas of society and culture, children of colour are often disadvantaged in the sphere of risky play. A study carried out in Nova Scotia found that Black children had more restricted access to risky play, partly due to racism and unsafe environments (Watson et al., 2023). In December 2022, statistically most UK children were back to their pre-pandemic levels of outdoor activity. However, there were clear inequalities, and Black children were still spending less time outside. We know that Black children are less likely to have access to green space and more likely to live in unsafe communities (Watkins, 2021). As mentioned previously, nine-year-old Ella Kissi-Debrah, who lived in London, was the first person in the world to have air pollution cited as a cause of death.

Black children often face higher levels of scrutiny and suspicion while playing in public spaces, and fear of violence or discrimination may discourage outdoor play and exploration.

Negative stereotypes about Black children can lead to over-policing and stricter supervision, limiting their freedom to engage in adventurous play activities. If we are aware of potential bias, we are more likely to avoid it.

Reflective question 17.4

In what ways can we advocate for and facilitate access to safe outdoor spaces and green areas for Black children, recognising the systemic inequalities that limit their opportunities for outdoor play and exploration?

Key takeaways

- Adopting a holistic approach to play that considers individual needs and challenges is crucial
- We must actively challenge gender stereotypes to promote non-gendered play
- It's important to recognise the importance of risky play for all children, including those with disabilities
- We must advocate for and facilitate access to safe and inclusive play environments for all children
- We need to continue to be reflective in order to improve our practice and support children's development

18

The role of the adult

Time and time again, when we ask children what needs to change to improve their lives, they tell us simply that they want to feel supported and listened to. This is not too much to ask.

Chollet et al., 2024

This chapter

- The importance of supporting and listening to children, keeping children safe through effective risk assessments, involving children in the risk assessment process
- The role of reflective practice, creating an emotionally supportive environment
- Using positive communication, and the significance of giving children time and trust to explore and take risks in play
- Understanding the importance of supporting and listening to children to improve their lives
- Exploring how to carry out effective risk assessments in play environments
- Recognising the value of involving children in the risk assessment process to enhance their decision-making skills and ownership
- Appreciating the role of reflective practice in evaluating and improving risk management strategies
- Understanding the significance of creating an emotionally supportive environment for children to take risks in play

(Continued)

- Exploring how positive spoken language and body language can build children's resilience and confidence
- Recognising the importance of giving children time and space to play and build trust in their abilities

Interacting or interfering?

In Early Years the role of the adult is primarily to facilitate and support, as opposed to planning and providing. We may have to manage aspects such as the time, breaks for rest and for food, but when it comes to play, the importance of our role lies less in our contributions. We do our best and most important work by being as unobtrusive as possible.

Have you ever noticed that the fastest way to stop children playing is to go and ask them what they're doing or attempt to join in? Most of the time there will be things the children actively request your involvement with, whether that be helping them, doing an activity with them or watching them while they show you their latest discovery or accomplishment. We live for these moments! Inviting yourself into their play, however – very bad form! I mean, they will always (usually) forgive you … but do you want to take the risk? In recent years the early learning community has got much better at this. We too have been through that process of learning to hold our comments where it doesn't actually add anything to their play, to slow down and observe and to think about our choice of language and vocabulary. That can be quite a challenge when you have grown up hearing 'be careful!' and 'mind you don't hurt yourself!' Let's spend a little time considering alternatives for these tired phrases that are, frankly, not very helpful!

Language

Considering that our focus is on play with an element of risk, we will have conducted our benefit–risk assessment for our site and our activities that may be undertaken. We are also practised in dynamically assessing for any additional hazards and determining risk that may arise through changes or new scenarios. As a result, our 'be careful!' could easily be developed into the far more helpful and specific 'be careful of …' and can be applied before children go off to play as well as a reminder where needed at key moments, should they arise. Still, can be used sparingly, we hope. At each point at which we feel we do need to provide input to their play experience, keep it brief, directed and specific – 'remember to check the branches are thicker than your wrist to stand on' or 'put the knife back into the sheath when you have finished with it'. Your input may be in the form of questions – 'have you checked those branches before you stand on them' or 'do you feel safe?' Asking them to reflect rather than giving an instruction is far more likely to result in them actually checking themselves. It also provides an opportunity for them to take responsibility for their decision-making and conduct their own assessment of the level of risk, which results in an increase in confidence and development in self-esteem. One of the greatest gifts we can give children is our trust. However brave and confident their exterior, though, we need to make sure they know it's OK to ask for help, so a simple 'I'm here if you need me' can be reassuring while not reducing their competency. We are the backstop, the *just in case*, the security and also their champion. 'I trust you'. Tuning into children's play and praising progress made can help them take risks in a healthy way. This coaching approach builds children's confidence and enables them to think critically. Our trust, praise and recognition of their achievements is incredibly valuable and should not be underestimated; through modelling this, children will in turn become each other's cheerleaders, support and role models.

> It was scary! It was the first time I climbed a tree! Cory helped me. He told me. He told me where I might go next. Are you proud?
>
> Joy, 5

As adults we are not immune from experiencing anxiety and concern when observing some risk in play. We may get a dose of adrenaline and suddenly feel more alert, with heightened senses. It helps if we acknowledge to ourselves how we are feeling. Children pick up on what we say, but they also pick up on our body language. We can build children's resilience and perseverance through positive language that helps them to feel strong and capable, so if we can take a deep breath and practise choosing and using more helpful language and phrases, that can also help us remain calm and model how to cope with these fears.

Here are some more examples of phrases or questions that could be employed when supporting children who are exploring their boundaries and capabilities with play and risk. Some are closed statements or questions, while others are more open-ended and give more room for reflection.

- Take your time.
- There's no hurry.
- Where will you put your foot next?
- If you need me, I am here.
- Test the branch with your foot – does it feel strong and stable?
- Try moving your foot to that branch.
- I like how you did …
- What will you hold onto?
- How can we stay safe in the hammock?

- Did you see that the rocks are slippery today?
- Watch out for children coming the other way.
- Remember our rule for carrying sticks.
- What is your plan?
- Do you see the …?
- Can you hear the …?

Figure 18.1 Supportive language can enable healthy risk-taking

Reflective questions 18.1

What types of questions and interactions do you find yourself using with children in your setting in these types of situations?

Do you share your favourite positive interactions with colleagues?

Relationships and interactions

In order to develop normally, a child requires progressively more complex joint activity with one or more adults who have an irrational emotional relationship with the child. Somebody's got to be crazy about that kid. That's number one. First, last, and always.

Urie Bronfenbrenner, 1979

The relationships we develop with the children we work with are absolutely at the root of our ability to manage risk and support children's need to explore this type of play. Trust is two-way, and how freely that is given also matters. We have to earn the trust of the children we work with (and their parents) through our respectful interactions, our genuine care and professional love and our belief in them. We need to trust that the children will rise to our expectations and our trust in them should be unequivocal, unless they give us reason for it not to be so. In almost every case they will either rise to it or show us the ways in which they need us to help them to develop the capability to achieve our expectations. Put simply, some children will need greater input than others. Some children will be more adept at assessing their own risks than others. Some will need more help in building up their confidence, as they may not be given opportunities to do things for themselves at home, may not be used to being trusted and what that means. Every interaction can make a child feel more or less capable or competent. Children want to be trusted to be autonomous in their play, but they need us to create an emotionally supportive environment.

Part of building a sense of competence is about stepping back if not needed and intervening only if it will benefit the child. It's important never to pressure a child to take a risk, but sometimes a child needs encouragement to step out of their comfort zone. If we always step in when children are involved in risky play, children can begin to doubt their abilities to deal with challenging situations. They get used to relying on an adult when deciding what to do and this can make them vulnerable in the future when they encounter other challenging situations. When deciding whether or when to step in, put the child at the centre of your thinking. Will they benefit from you stepping in? Do they want you to? Do they need you to? Be available and present without taking over.

> Playworkers choose an intervention style that enables children and young people to extend their play. All playworker interventions must balance risk with the developmental benefit and wellbeing of children.
>
> Play Wales, 2005

If a child does become anxious or 'stuck', it's important not to pressurise them. If they change their mind, reassure them that that's fine. You could:

- celebrate the progress the child has made so far;
- let the child know you are there if needed;
- acknowledge how the child is feeling. When there is risk in play, emotions such as anxiety or fear are more likely and young children can find these feelings very hard to deal with. Talk through these feelings together;
- listen carefully to what the child is saying and read the child's body language;
- ask open-ended questions such as 'how do you feel?' (You may want to link this to physical sensations – 'how do you feel in your tummy?');
- ask another child to have a go at the challenge so you can watch and discuss together;

- help the child self-instruct. Psychologist Lev Vygotsky (1962) observed that young children often talk out loud as they work out a problem. We can model this process and support children with this.

Table 18.1 Stages of self-instruction

Stage		Example
Problem definition	The child works out what the challenge is	'I want to make a tall tower with this puppet on the top'
Focusing attention/ planning	The child starts to make a plan	'I could put these blocks on the cable reel. I could climb on there to get higher'
Strategy	The child explains how to engage and use a strategy	'Jack and me will work together to stand on the reel and pile the blocks on'
Self-evaluation	The child detects errors and corrects	'There's not enough room on the reel so we have to take it in turns'
Coping	The child learns to deal with challenges and failures	'The blocks were falling down, but we found a new way'
Self-reinforcement	The child rewards themselves for accomplishments	'We made the tallest tower'

Note: Stages conceived by Graham et al. (1992), inspired by Vygotsky (1962).

> A key aim is to support children to develop their decision-making skills, rather than taking the decision-making out of their hands. It can be tempting to step in and solve problems for children who are struggling in the outdoor environment, especially when time is an issue, but we need to be careful that our impatience doesn't prevent children from learning to navigate difficulties.
>
> Watkins, 2021, p. 34

The book *Interacting or Interfering?* by Julie Fisher (2016) discusses that, in order to be effective, an interaction needs to enhance the child's learning or development. However, adults sometimes impose their own agendas on children. When we dominate the interactions, we interfere with the learning process. Knowing when to intervene and when to step back is crucial, but can be difficult to judge. Fisher urges us to tune into children, be sensitive to the learning possibilities of an interaction and adjust accordingly. Stillness, observation, listening and thinking are vital. If a child is in immediate danger, we know to step in straight away. If not, waiting, watching and wondering allow us to decide whether to step in or not. Our relationships with each individual child should inform our decisions.

Time is a crucial element here and if, as practitioners, we feel pressured, we are less likely to be able to take the time to support children to learn the skills they need to risk assess, evaluate and problem solve. Children need time and space to challenge themselves.

> At Forest School, it's not like school. You don't have to rush to get your work done. It's like children's time.
>
> Jon, 9

Unfortunately, the way that the curriculum is interpreted in some settings means that taking the time to build relationships with children is not always valued (Watkins, 2021). When children can immerse themselves in play, uninterrupted, they are in a good place to begin to challenge themselves and increase the complexity of their play. Children need time and space to let the play process take over.

Reflective question 18.2

How do you gauge when your intervention is truly necessary for children's benefit, rather than impeding their learning process?

Figure 18.2 Relationships are key to risk-taking

Co-explorers

The grown-ups at playtime just chat. I don't think they like break time. We did have one teacher who liked coming outside and playing even when it was raining, but she was from college, I think. She's gone now.

George, 8

I vividly remember a colleague walking past when I was outside with a group of children and commenting: 'I don't know who is the biggest child – you or them!' Initially, I felt offended, but it also made me think. Working at a university, I draw effectively on my sense of curiosity all the time. I'm an invested co-explorer when working with children because I'm genuinely fascinated to rediscover an environment through co-play.

Collaboration characterises all of my work, whether working with a dance company, a literary festival, a group of teachers or a group of children. Risk in play is often collaborative and is most successful when an adult is genuinely interested in the journey of a child, as they move out of their comfort zone and into the growth zone. Sadly, research shows us that parents and carers are increasingly less present when children are playing, which makes our role as collaborators and co-explorers even more crucial.

The role of reflection

When I sit in the sit spot at Forest School, it's good to think about all the things around me. It helps me focus and concentrate.

Vanessa, 11

I remember a four-year-old girl in my class who often felt unsuccessful in terms of phonics and other 'academic' areas. This child was initially extremely anxious about entering the Forest School area. She visibly trembled when walking on the uneven ground. With encouragement and regular exposure to the area over a number of weeks, she became confident enough to eventually climb a small slope that had always intimidated her (this was a challenge she became desperate to meet). She was keen to discuss this achievement with all the adults in the setting over and over again. Reflecting on her progress in this area built her resilience in other areas and boosted her self-esteem.

Before she successfully tackled this physical challenge, this child 'failed' over and over again. It was an important process for her to reflect on the small steps of progress that she made, such as walking through the long grass. These were all steps on her journey.

When children are supported to play in risky ways, it's important that adults have the opportunity to discuss progress made by the children and talk through challenges experienced by staff.

Expectations: trusting the process

We can help children develop the tools to meet our expectations if we help them build resilience. A child who is not given responsibility will struggle to take responsibility – it is something of a self-fulfilling prophecy. Looking again at the language we use: a child struggling to meet expectations or achieve any significant challenge might say 'I can't' or 'it's too hard'. Our trusting response could be 'you can do hard things'. We don't detract from the fact it is hard or challenging, but we still believe them to be capable, and we are there to support them if they need us.

This time taken to build these relationships and to become fully absorbed in developing skills (of all types and at all levels, not only those with an element of risk, but anything which captures their interest, attention and imagination) is vital. The theme of the importance of childhood as a time to be nurtured and preserved, protected and valued has recurred since Froebelian times, at least. One of the Froebelian principles is the value of childhood in its own right: 'Childhood is not merely a preparation for the next stage in learning. Learning begins at birth and continues throughout life' (Froebel, n.d.). We should avoid a focus on 'getting ready to move on' – whether that be a 'rising threes' stage, where the two-year-olds are celebrated and cheered on for being 'nearly three' instead of being celebrated just for being two; or the pre-school children are encouraged to look ahead to when they will start school. Froebel was telling us that this time of being a child, and indeed each stage of childhood, should not be seen as a *level* to achieve in order to move on to the next, but should rather be valued for its own sake. In order to do that we must appreciate all of the moments, all of the time spent learning and not rush through them.

Reflective questions 18.3

How do you cultivate an environment of trust with the children in your care?

Are you conscious of taking time with this process, or does it sometimes feel rushed? How can we slow down time?

Slow pedagogy

At the start of this book, we explored the way that David Elkind, in his book *Hurried Child* (1981), discussed the pressures society put on children to grow up too fast. I'm sure we can all think of examples, both from our own childhood and possibly that we ourselves might have suggested as we naturally absorbed this cultural message – 'I need you to be big and brave'; 'X is for babies, you're a big boy/girl now'; expecting children to take increasing responsibility as economic changes means fewer stay-at-home parents; children expected to be more independent; ... we can see the patterns.

Professor Alison Clark (2023), through her research on the importance of a slow, unhurried childhood where we put the child firmly back at the centre and focus entirely on their needs and interests, brings us the term 'slow pedagogy'. Her initial research study was concluded in 2021 and her work reminds us that as the adults we can help to slow down time for our children. When they go to their care setting, that time is theirs; they should not have every part of it planned or mapped out for them. We should be observing and being guided by their pace and rhythm, supporting children to revisit themes and ideas that captivate them as often as they need to, or going deeper into their learning, as with the different play types, especially deep play. With conscious focus, we can bring about routines which are unhurried and allow connections – to each other, between children and adults and to the environment. With a focus on play with an element of risk, it is only good sense not to feel rushed, but to have time to engage in the activity safely and in an unhurried way. The pressures on Early Years teachers and practitioners have grown enormously in recent years, becoming more checklist- and data-driven and demanding. This reminder and validation of the benefits of a slow pedagogical approach is surely of benefit to all of us, not only the children.

Supporting babies and very young children

What about working with babies and very young children? There is perhaps nothing that slows down time quite like cuddling babies! But what does risky play look like for babies and younger toddlers? The riskiest (not really, but possibly the first thing that requires baby to explore and test their confidence and can be a bit scary) is learning to walk. It's a huge milestone moment, those first steps! (When reading that, did you immediately reflect back on the slow pedagogy paragraph above and think about how adults often put so much emphasis on getting to this point? I know I did.) But, when baby is ready – and the beauty of this is it really doesn't matter whether an adult thinks they 'should' be walking, most children get there in their own time – we can help to make those first steps both exciting, interesting, challenging and just as safe as necessary. Once a baby is up, usually having pulled themselves up on a fixed piece of furniture, they need to work out how to get down again. At first, they may just let go of the furniture and fall down with a bump or have a momentary panic that they don't know what to do and cry for help. This is all part of the learning process and carers can help by showing a baby how to bend their legs and lower themselves to the ground without getting hurt. This also really helps to ease falls when babies start taking steps independently. If we do this from a hands-off position, we are letting the little one know 'you can do this' and 'I'm here to help you'. Lots of praise and championing language can help them gain the confidence that this scary thing is not beyond them.

Outdoors is a great place for first steps to happen – if they can do this scary thing in this big, open space, then indoors looks much easier. Being outdoors boosts endorphins and if baby is feeling happier this in turn feeds their confidence. Ideally, babies will learn to walk barefoot, as the increased connection with the ground helps them to feel more stable and to grip more easily. It's worth considering if you can make your outdoor space safe enough for this. Having a number of secure structures that babies and little ones can pull up on can really help as they will want to explore the different areas. As they grow in confidence, different levels and textures help to challenge their new and emerging balance and confidence. Babies who have been swung and moved in different directions (including, even especially, upside down) in games and play, in ways that challenge their vestibular system early on, will find this much easier and less stressful, so practitioners can ensure that they receive that input. Finally, when it comes to how much we support them in taking those physical steps, let's try not to be helicopters, hovering with our arms up as if expecting them to fall and need catching. If we have ensured the space and surfaces are safe (enough), and they are pulling themselves up to standing, trust that they've got this. Next stop – the wobbly bridge!

That brings me, finally, to the idea of graduated challenges – providing the physical environment that will facilitate every child of all age groups to progress, to continue to develop their skills.

Case study: risk in play and attachment by John Stuart

Today's society is arguably the most risk-averse it ever has been. Adults have shaped this cultural attitude through a whole variety of well-intentioned means that have produced a plethora of unintended consequences for child development. Outdoor play is a modality that synthesises *play* with the *outdoor* setting. This pedagogical approach brings with it unique potentialities for optimal holistic child development, arguably due to the risk the context provides.

Having a secure attachment is at the root of optimal child development. As practitioners it would be sensible to consider the developmental implications for children and young people engaging in play with an element of risk through the lens of attachment theory. To do this, we turn specifically to one of the core concepts of attachment theory, the *safe base*. The safe base is a construct of the child's experience of the physical and emotional sensitivity and responsiveness of their caregivers, particularly during times of anxiety or distress. As children experience these sensitive and responsive relationships, they learn to trust in the availability and reliability of them which facilitates their capacity to explore beyond the safety of their immediate world. The concept of the *secure* base is so important in the context of play with an

(Continued)

element of risk, as it directly links attachment with exploration, which, as a matter of course, involves risk-taking.

Play, with an element of risk, particularly in an outdoor setting, provides the context in which the psychological construct of the safe base can be prioritised, developed and strengthened on an individual basis. The presence of risk in play sets the optimal conditions for the child to test the limits of their current anxieties while developing in them the resilience and curiosity to explore further. Risk, therefore, becomes a significant mediator in the development of the safe base, while play provides the protective scaffolding required to optimise it. Experience of risk in play cues our response to provide safety as caregivers and for our children to seek comfort. The element of risk in play should not be shied away from; instead it should be embraced for its capacity to influence child development optimally and from its core.

Key takeaways

- It's important to adopt a comprehensive approach to risk management that involves the children
- Involve children in the decision-making
- It is crucial to know when to step in and when to step back to support children's independence and problem-solving skills
- Using positive communication and emotional support builds children's resilience and confidence in risky play
- We need to ensure that play environments are safe yet conducive to risk-taking and exploration

References

Adolph, K. E., Kretch, K. S. and LoBue, V. (2014) Fear of heights in infants? *Current Directions in Psychological Science*, 23(1), 60–6. https://doi.org/10.1177/0963721413498895

Änggård, E. (2011) Children's gendered and non-gendered play in natural spaces. *Children, Youth and Environments*, 21(2), 5–33. Available at: www.researchgate.net/publication/259751120_Children's_Gendered_and_Non-Gendered_Play_in_Natural_Spaces (accessed 27 November 2024).

Anji Play (n.d.) *Principles and Practices*. Available at: www.anjiplay.com/principles-and-practices (accessed 10 October 2024).

Arnold, J. C. (2014) *Their Name is Today: Reclaiming Childhood in a Hostile World*. New York: Plough.

Aunt Annie's Childcare (n.d.) *Turning Parents on to Risky Play*. Available at: https://auntannieschildcare.blogspot.com/2012/03/turning-parents-on-to-risky-play.html (accessed 10 October 2024).

Baines, E. and Blatchford, P. (2023) The decline in breaktimes and lunchtimes in primary and secondary schools in England: results from three national surveys spanning 25 years. *British Educational Research Journal*. Available at: https://doi.org/10.1002/berj.3874 (accessed 27 November 2024).

Ball, D. (2007) Risk and the demise of children's play. In B. Thom, R. Sales and J. Pearce (eds), *Growing Up with Risk*. Bristol: Policy Press. Policy Press Scholarship Online edn, 22 March 2012. Available at: https://doi.org/10.1332/policypress/9781861347329.003.0004 (accessed 9 October 2024).

Beames, S., Higgins, P., Nicol, M. and Smith, H. (2024) *Outdoor Learning Across the Curriculum*. London: Routledge.

Bottrill, G. (2018) *Can I Go and Play Now?* London: Sage.

Bowlby, J. (1988) *A Secure Base*. London: Routledge.

Bronfenbrenner, U. (1979) *The Ecology of Human Development: Experiments by Nature and Design*. Cambridge, MA: Harvard University Press.

Brown, S. (2009) *Play is More than Just Fun* [video]. TED Conferences. Available at: www.ted.com/talks/stuart_brown_play_is_more_than_just_fun (accessed 27 November 2024).

Bruce, T. (2012) *Early Childhood Practice: Froebel Today*. London: Sage.

Brussoni, M., Gibbons, R., Gray, C., Ishikawa, T., Sandseter, E. B., Bienenstock, A., Chabot, G., Fuselli, P., Herrington, S., Janssen, I., Pickett, W., Power, M., Stanger, N., Sampson, M. and Tremblay, M. S. (2015) What is the relationship between risky outdoor play and health in children? A systematic review. *International Journal of Environmental Research and Public Health*, 12(6), 6423–54.

Brussoni, M., Olsen, L. L., Pike, I. and Sleet, D. A. (2012) Risky play and children's safety: balancing priorities for optimal child development. *International Journal of Environmental Research and Public Health*, 9(9), 3134–48.

Bryson, T. and Siegal, D. (2012) *The Whole-Brain Child*. London: Little, Brown.

BSI Group (1986) BS 5696:1986 Specification for Playground Equipment. CEN, 1998. EN 1176–1:1998 Playground Equipment and Surfacing – Part 1: General Safety Requirements and Test Methods. London: BSI.

Buchan, N. (2018) *Adventurous Play*. London: Teaching Solutions.

Bundy, A., Luckett, T., Tranter, P., Naughton, G., Wyver, S., Ragen, J. and Spies, G. (2009) The risk is that there is 'no risk': a simple, innovative intervention to increase children's activity levels. *International Journal of Early Years Education*, 17(1), 33-45

Caprino, F. (2018) When the risk is worth it: the inclusion of children with disabilities in free risky play. National Institute for Documentation, Innovation and Educational Research. Available at: www.researchgate.net/publication/338067931_When_the_risk_is_worth_it_the_inclusion_of_children_with_disabilities_in_free_risky_play (accessed 28 November 2024).

Care Inspectorate (2021) Keeping children safe poster artwork, SIMOA. Available at: https://hub.careinspectorate.com/media/4530/keeping-children-safe-poster-artwork-simoa.pdf (accessed 10 October 2024).

Chollet, D., Turner, A., Marquez, J., O'Neill, J. and Moore, L. (2024) *The Good Childhood Report 2024*. Available at: www.childrenssociety.org.uk/information/professionals/resources/good-childhood-report-2024 (accessed 10 October 2024).

Clark, A. (2017) *Listening to Young Children*. London: Jessica Kingsley.

Clark, A. (2023) *Slow Knowledge and the Unhurried Child: Time for Slow Pedagogies in Early Childhood Education*. Abingdon: Routledge.

Dahl, R. (1993) *Roald Dahl: My Year*. London: Jonathan Cape.

Department for Education and Department of Health (DfE and DHSC) (2015) *SEND Code of Practice: 0 to 25 Years*. Available at: www.gov.uk/government/publications/send-code-of-practice-0-to-25 (accessed 28 November 2024).

Dodd, H. (2022) *Adventurous Play: A Prevention for Anxiety*. Podcast for the Association for Child and Adolescent Mental Health (ACAMH). Available at: https://acamhlearn.org/Learning/Adventurous_Play%3A_A_Prevention_For_Anxiety/b402ac14-e01c-440b-ae3f-f41328976dad (accessed 28 November 2024).

Dodd, H. and Lester, K. (2021) Adventurous play as a mechanism for reducing risk for childhood anxiety: a conceptual model. *Clinical Child and Family Psychology Review*, 24, 164–81.

Dodd, H. F., FitzGibbon, L., Watson, B. E. and Nesbit, R. J. (2021) Children's play and independent mobility in 2020: Results from the British Children's Play Survey. *International Journal of Environmental Research and Public Health*, 18(8), 4334. https://doi.org/10.3390/ijerph18084334

Dr Seuss (1954) *Horton Hears a Who!* New York: Random House.

Eager, D. and Little, H. (2011) *Risk Deficit Disorder* [Parks and Leisure Australia National Conference 2011]. University of Technology Sydney, Australia; Macquarie University, Australia.

Early Years Coalition (EYC) (2021) *Birth to 5 Matters: Non-statutory Guidance to the Early Years Foundation Stage*. Available at: https://birthto5matters.org.uk/wp-content/uploads/2021/03/Birthto5Matters-download.pdf (accessed 10 October 2024).

Education Scotland (2020) *Realising the Ambition, Being Me*. Produced for the Education Scotland by APS Group Scotland. Available at: https://education.gov.scot/media/3bjpr3wa/realisingtheambition.pdf (accessed 28 November 2024).

Elkind, D. (1981) *Hurried Child: Growing Up Too Fast Too Soon*. Reading: Addison-Wesley.

Elsley, S. (2015) *Play Map: A Resource for Community Planning Partnerships*. Available at: https://hub.careinspectorate.com/media/1295/play-map-a-resource-for-community-planning-partnerships.pdf (accessed 9 October 2024).

Fawcett Society (2020) *Unlimited Potential: Report of the Commission on Gender Stereotypes in Early Childhood*. Available at: www.fawcettsociety.org.uk/ (accessed 10 October 2024).

Fisher, J. (2016) *Interacting or Interfering? Improving Interactions in the Early Years*. Maidenhead: Open University Press.

Forest School Training in England and Scotland (FSTC) (n.d.) *Forest School Overview*. Available at: www.forestschooltraining.co.uk/forest-school/ (accessed 9 October 2024).

Froebel, F. (1887) *The Education of Man*. Trans. W. N. Hailmann. New York: D. Appleton & Company Press (original work published 1826). https://doi.org/10.1037/12739-000

Froebel Trust (n.d.) Froebel Trust. Available at: www.froebel.org.uk/ (accessed 10 October 2024).

Frost, J. L. (2010) *A History of Children's Play and Play Environments: Toward a Contemporary Child-Saving Movement*. New York: Routledge.

George's Fund (n.d.) George's Fund. Available at: www.georgesfund.co.uk/ (accessed 10 October 2024).

Gibson, J. J. (1977) The theory of affordances. In R. Shaw and J. Bransford (eds), *Perceiving, Acting, and Knowing: Toward an Ecological Psychology*. Hillsdale, NJ: Erlbaum, pp. 67–82.

Gill, T. (2007) *No Fear: Growing Up in a Risk Averse Society*. London: Calouste Gulbenkian Foundation.

Gill, T., Power, M. and Brussoni, M. (2019) *Risk Benefit Assessment for Outdoor Play: A Canadian Toolkit*. Ottawa: Child and Nature Alliance of Canada. Available at: https://indd.adobe.com/view/44ed054b-917b-4e02-a1e3-e6c4cbfe0360 (accessed 28 November 2024).

Gladstone, A. and Rice, G. (2016) *We're OK with Risky Play!* New York: Lawrence Educational.

Graham, S., Harris, K. R. and Reid, R. (1992) Developing self-regulated learners. *Focus on Exceptional Children*, 24, 1–16.

Gray, P. (2013) *Free to Learn: Why Unleashing the Instinct to Play Will Make Our Children Happier, More Self-Reliant, and Better Prepared for Life*. New York: Basic Books.

Gray, P. (2014) Risky play: why children love it and need it. *Psychology Today*. Available at: www.psychologytoday.com/gb/blog/freedom-learn/201404/risky-play-why-children-love-it-and-need-it (accessed 28 November 2024).

Gregory, A. (2024) Myopia will affect 740m children and teenagers by 2050, research suggests. *Guardian*. Available at: www.theguardian.com/society/2024/sep/24/myopia-will-affect-740m-children-and-teenagers-by-2050-research-suggests (accessed 9 October 2024).

Hanscom, A. (2016) *Balanced and Barefoot*. Oakland, CA: New Harbinger.

Health and Safety Executive (HSE) (2012) *Children's Play and Leisure: Promoting a Balanced Approach*. Available at: www.hse.gov.uk/entertainment/assets/docs/childrens-play-july-2012.pdf (accessed 4 December 2024).

Hedlund, J. (2000) Risky business: safety regulations, risk compensation, and individual behavior. *Injury Prevention*, 6(2), 82–9. https://doi.org/10.1136/ip.6.2.82

Henderson, T. R. (2020) *The Springtime of the People: The Athenian Ephebeia and Citizen Training from Lykourgos to Augustus*. Leiden, The Netherlands: Brill. https://doi.org/10.1163/9789004433366

Holland, C. (2009) *I Love My World*. Devon: Wholeland Press.

Holland, P. (2003) *We Don't Play with Guns Here*. London: Open University Press.

Hughes, B. (2006) *A Playworker's Taxonomy of Play Types*. London: Playlink.

International Play Association (IPA) (2013) *This Is Me: Article 31 and a Child's Right to Play*. Available at: www.youtube.com/watch?v=5tjRPWPhIfA (accessed 9 October 2024).

IPA (n.d.a) Article 31 for Children. Home resources for children, poster. Available at: https://ipaworld.org/resources/for-children/article-31-for-children/ (accessed 9 October 2024).

IPA (n.d.b) Complete Council home, *About Us*. Available at: https://ipaworld.org/about-us/complete-council/ (accessed 9 October 2024).

ISO (2023) ISO 4980:2023(en) *Benefit–Risk Assessment for Sports and Recreational Facilities, Activities and Equipment*. Available at: www.iso.org/obp/ui/en/#iso:std:iso:4980:ed-1:v1:en (accessed 10 October 2024).

Jarvis, P. and Liebovich, B. (2015) British nurseries, head and heart: McMillan, Owen and the genesis of the education/care dichotomy. *Women's History Review*, 24(6), 917–37. https://doi.org/10.1080/09612025.2015.1025662

Kleppe, R., Melhuish, E. and Beate Hansen Sandseter, E. (2017) Identifying and characterizing risky play in the age one-to-three years. *European Early Childhood Education Research Journal*, 25(3), 370–85. https://doi.org/10.1080/1350293X.2017.1308163

Kochanowski, L. and Carr, V. (2014) Nature playscapes as contexts for fostering self-determination. *Children, Youth and Environments*, 24(2), 146. https://doi.org/10.7721/chilyoutenvi.24.2.0146

Liebschner, J. (1992) *A Child's Work: Freedom and Guidance in Froebel's Educational Theory and Practice*. Cambridge: Lutterworth Press.

Lindon, J. (1999) *Too Safe for Their Own Good?* London: Jessica Kingsley.

Little, H. and Eager, D. (2010) Risk, challenge and safety: Implications for play quality and playground design. *European Early Childhood Education Research Journal*, 18, 497–513. https://doi.org/10.1080/1350293X.2010.525949

Louv, R. (2010) *Last Child in the Woods*. London: Atlantic.

Lowry, C. A., Hollis, J. H., de Vries, A., Pan, B., Brunet, L. R., Hunt, J. R., Paton, J. F., van Kampen, E., Knight, D. M., Evans, A. K., Rook, G. A. and Lightman, S. L. (2007) Identification of an immune-responsive mesolimbocortical serotonergic system: Potential role in regulation of emotional behavior. *Neuroscience*, 146(2), 756–72. doi: 10.1016/j.neuroscience.2007.01.067

Lynch, H., Moore, A., Edwards, C. and Horgan, L. (2018) *Community Parks and Playgrounds: Intergenerational Participation through Universal Design. Final Report*. Available at: https://nda.ie/uploads/publications/Community-Parks-and-Playgrounds-Universal-Design-RPS2017.pdf (accessed 10 October 2024).

Martin, C. L. and Ruble, D. N. (2010) Patterns of gender development. *Annual Review of Psychology*, 61, 353–81. https://doi.org/10.1146/annurev.psych.093008.100511

Meehan, R. J. (2010) *Teacher's Journey*. London: Tate.

Milne, A. A. and Shepard, E. H. (1928) *The House at Pooh Corner*. London: Methuen.

Montessori, M. (1986) *The Discovery of the Child*. Amsterdam: Montessori-Pierson.

Moorhouse, P. (2018) *Learning Through Woodwork: Introducing Creative Woodwork in the Early Years* London: Routledge.

Morrongiello, B. A., Zdzieborski, D. and Normand, J. (2010) Understanding gender differences in children's risk taking and injury: a comparison of mothers' and fathers' reactions to sons and daughters misbehaving in ways that lead to injury. *Journal of Applied Developmental Psychology*, 31(4), 322–9. https://doi.10.1016/j.appdev.2010.05.004

Mortari, L. and Zerbato, R. (2007/8) Avventure in Natura [Adventures in Nature]. *Edizioni Junior*. Trans. I. Micheli. Edinburgh: Children in Scotland.

Newstead, S. (2016) *The Busker's Guide to Risk*. London: Jessica Kingsley.

Omer, H. (2017) *Parental Vigilant Care: A Guide for Clinicians and Caretakers*. New York: Routledge.

OPAL (n.d.) *Outdoor Play and Learning*. Available at: https://outdoorplayandlearning.org.uk/ (accessed 28 November 2024).

Outdoor Risky Play for All (2013) Blog. Available at : https://earlyyearsoutdooreducation.wordpress.com/outdoor-risky-play-for-all/ (accessed 12 December 2024).

Outdoor Woodland Learning Scotland (OWLS) (2024) *Fire Guidance*. Available at: https://owlscotland.org/resources/fire-guidance (accessed 10 October 2024).

Pemberton, L. (n.d.) The Black Nursery Manager. Available at: www.theblacknurserymanager.com/ (accessed 5 December 2024).

Play England (n.d.a) *Charter for Play*. Available at: www.playengland.org.uk/charter-for-play (accessed 9 October 2024).

Play England (n.d.b) *Play in England: A New 10-Year Strategy*. Available at: www.playengland.org.uk/strategy (accessed 9 October 2024).

Play Safety Forum (2008) *Managing Risk in Play Provision: A Position Statement*. Available at: https://playsafetyforum.wordpress.com/wp-content/uploads/2015/03/managing-risk-in-play-provision-position-statement.pdf (accessed 9 October 2024).

Play Scotland (2023) *Getting it Right for Play: The Power of Play: An Evidence Base*. Available at: www.playscotland.org/resources/getting-it-right-for-play/ (accessed 9 October 2024).

Play Wales (2005) *The Playwork Principles*. Available at: https://play.wales/playwork/the-playwork-principles/ (accessed 10 October 2024).

Play Wales (2023) *This is Why Play is So Important*. Available at: https://play.wales/news/play-wales-news/new-film-this-is-why-play-is-so-important/ (accessed 2 December 2024).

PlayBoard NI (2024) PlayBoard NI. Available at: www.playboard.org/ (accessed 9 October 2024).

Playful Childhoods (2023) *This is Why Play is So Important*. Available at: www.youtube.com/watch?v=UnfdamgVFhY&t=2s&ab_channel=PlayfulChildhoods (accessed 28 November 2024).

Rewilding Britain (n.d.) *Defining Rewilding*. Available at: www.rewildingbritain.org.uk/why-rewild/what-is-rewilding/an-introduction-to-rewilding/defining-rewilding (accessed 10 October 2024).

Reynolds, K. (2014) *Perceptions of Childhood*. Online, British Library. Available at: www.britishlibrary.cn/en/articles/perceptions-of-childhood/#:~:text=In%20the%20mid%2D18th%20century,they%20could%20preserve%20childhood%20indefinitely (accessed 28 November 2024).

Ryan, R. M. and Deci, E. L. (2000) Self-determination theory and the facilitation of intrinsic motivation, social development, and well-being. *American Psychologist*, 55(1), 68–78. doi:10.1037/0003-066X.55.1.68

Sanders, K. Y. (2006) Overprotection and lowered expectations of persons with disabilities: the unforeseen consequences. *Work*, 27(2), 181–8.

Sandseter, E. B. H. (2007) Categorising risky play: how can we identify risk-taking in children's play? *European Early Childhood Education Research Journal*, 15(2), 237–52. https://doi.org/10.1080/13502930701321733

Sandseter, E. B. H. (2010) Scaryfunny: a qualitative study of risky play among preschool children. Doctoral thesis. Norwegian University of Science and Technology, Trondheim.

Sandseter, E. B. H. and Kennair, L. E. O. (2011) Children's risky play from an evolutionary perspective: the anti-phobic effects of thrilling experiences. *Evolutionary Psychology*, 9(2), 257–84.

Scottish Executive (2004) *A Curriculum for Excellence*. Available at: www.education-uk.org/documents/pdfs/2004-scottish-curriculum-review.pdf (accessed 10 March 2025)

Scottish Parliament (2024) United Nations Convention on the Rights of the Child (Incorporation) (Scotland) Bill. Available at: www.parliament.scot/bills-and-laws/bills/s5/united-nations-convention-on-the-rights-of-the-child-incorporation-scotland-bill (accessed 9 October 2024).

Shakespeare, T. (2004) Social models of disability and other life strategies. *Scandinavian Journal of Disability Research*, 6(1), 8–21. https://doi.org/10.1080/15017410409512636

Solly, K. (2014) *Risk, Challenge and Adventure in the Early Years*. London: Routledge.

Sinek, S. (2009) *Start with Why*. London: Penguin.

Souri, H. and Hasanirad, T. (2011) Relationship between resilience, optimism and psychological well-being in students of Medicine. *Procedia: Social and Behavioral Sciences*, 30, 1541–4.

Spinka, M., Newberry, R. C. and Bekoff, M. (2001) Mammalian play: training for the unexpected. *Quarterly Review of Biology*, 76(2), 141–68. https://doi.org/10.1086/393866

Spock, B. (1946) *Baby and Child Care*. New York: Duell, Sloan and Pearce.

Stevinson, E. (1954) *Margaret McMillan: Prophet and Pioneer*. London: University of London Press.

Stewart, I. (2017) Danny MacAskill's mum: 'I never worry about my son's stunts'. *BBC News*. Available at: www.bbc.co.uk/news/uk-scotland-41280170 (accessed 28 November 2024).

Thrive Outdoors (2020) *A Practitioner's Guide to Outdoor Play Based Learning*. Available at: www.inspiringscotland.org.uk/wp-content/uploads/2020/07/Practitioner-Tips-What-to-Wear-THRIVE_.pdf (accessed 10 October 2024).

Topping, A. (2016) Girls as young as 7 feel pressure to be pretty: body confidence study. *Guardian*. Available at: www.theguardian.com/lifeandstyle/2016/oct/04/girls-as-young-as-7-feel-pressure-to-be-pretty-body-confidence-girlguiding-study-reveals (accessed 10 October 2024).

Tyrie, J., Sarwar, S., Dumitrscu, S., Mannello, M., Haughton, C., Ellis, C. and Connolly, M. (2019) Power, rights and play: control of play in school grounds, an action research project from Wales. *Education 3–13*, 47(6), 627–36.

Ulich, R., Lilley, I. M. and Froebel, F. (1968) Friedrich Froebel: a selection from his writings. *History of Education Quarterly*, 8(4), 528. https://doi.org/10.2307/367544

UN (1989) *The United Nations Convention on the Rights of the Child*. Treaty no. 27531. United Nations Treaty Series, 1577, pp. 3–178. Available at: www.unicef.org.uk/wp-content/uploads/2016/08/unicef-convention-rights-child-uncrc.pdf (accessed 28 November 2024).

UN Committee on the Rights of the Child (2013) United Nations General Comment No. 17. Available at: https://ipaworld.org/wp-content/uploads/2013/11/IPA-Summary-of-UN-GC-article-31_FINAL1.pdf (accessed 9 October 2024).

UNICEF (2024) *Rights Respecting Schools*. Available at: www.unicef.org.uk/rights-respecting-schools/ (accessed 10 October 2024).

Vygotsky, L. (1962) *Thought and Language*. Cambridge, MA: MIT Press (original work published 1934).

Wainwright, A. (1973) *A Coast to Coast Walk*. Kendal: Westmorland Gazette.

Wall, T. (2020) The new road rage: bitter rows break out over UK's low-traffic neighbourhoods. *Guardian*. Available at: www.theguardian.com/world/2020/sep/20/the-new-road-rage-bitter-rows-break-out-over-uks-low-traffic-neighbourhoods (accessed 9 October 2024).

Watkins, S. (2021) *Outdoor Play for Healthy Little Minds: Practical Ideas to Promote Children's Wellbeing in the Early Years*. Little Minds Matter. London: Routledge.

Watson, C., Stirling Cameron, E., Hickens, N., Pimentel, M., Hamilton-Hinch, B. and McIsaac, J. L. D. (2023) Early childhood leisure experiences of African Nova Scotian children: the privilege of risky outdoor play. *Leisure/Loisir*, 48(2), 211–29.

Wright, B., Bahnimptewa, C. and Heard Museum (2014) *Kachinas: A Hopi Artist's Documentary, by Barton Wright*. New foreword by Ann Marshall; original paintings by Clifford Bahnimptewa. New Mexico: Museum of New Mexico Press.

Index

Zeitfracht Medien GmbH
Ferdinand-Jühlke-Straße 7
99095 Erfurt, Deutschland
produktsicherheit@kolibri360.de